Your Profound Success

7 Powerful Ways to Skyrocket Your Business Using the Internet

Dear Heather,

LIVE PROFOUND!

Amit

Amit Ambegaonkar & Raymond Aaron

Publisher
10-10-10 Publishing
Markham, ON
Canada

Your Profound Success

ISBN:

Printed in Canada and the United States of America

Contents

Dedication

I dedicate my book to you, the aspiring entrepreneur, as you use this book to help you determine your path to success.

I want to encourage you through my book to achieve your success, as you have chosen the path to be an entrepreneur. This path is challenging but is ultimately rewarding, if you keep moving in the right direction and if you do not give up.

I understand that the journey may be long and lonely or even sometimes give you a feeling of 'why did I do this'?

However, my friend, if you keep defining your purpose and focusing on your goals you will keep discovering new reasons why you want to do this.

So start with a great mindset, accept your challenges and let's achieve more not only for ourselves but also for the people that need us and will benefit from what we have to offer!

Testimonials

"This book is a must read to attract the abundance you deserve online! Guide yourself through these pages to structure your business with the vital sequential steps you need. I congratulate you Amit for writing this incredible book and helping so many entrepreneurs to fulfill their dreams and helping them to reach their goal of financial freedom."

~ Mike Schryer
CEO - i Inspire Inc.

"Amit Ambegaonkar gives us a powerful and strategic online blueprint to build the critical yet necessary components to successfully upscale our online presence and marketing growth, for your profound solutions. Amit reveals the truth that real wealth is achievable and available to all the Entrepreneurs, that he teaches, coaches and trains -using his systems and practical methods, that will surely stand the test of time!"

~ Valerie Kanay
Award Winning Authorities Author and Host, "The Rich Flow of Life" pod cast

"Amit is a successful entrepreneur and hence understands your challenges and problems as an entrepreneur. Through his proven system, he empowers you to gain enormous success in your business. In this book, Amit lays out a very structured plan for you to carry out so that you can scale your business to soaring heights."

~ Vishal Morjaria
Award Winning Author and Transformational Speaker

"This is a must-read book for entrepreneurs wanting to get their businesses positioned with the big players online – above the fold on Google! Amit is an award winning author, and a knowledgeable and responsive business and online coach. Amit Ambegaonkar is some one to watch."

~ Heather F Edgington
Dream Builder Coach

Acknowledgements

First and foremost, I would like to acknowledge my mentor and my coach, Mr. Raymond Aaron for giving me direction in my life and teaching me the right things at the right time. Raymond you are one of the most influential person in my life.

I would like to thank my parents, Late Mr. Dilip M. Ambegaonkar and Mrs. Vijaya Ambegaonkar for supporting me and nurturing me in a very special way. Your love and care have made it possible for me to be what I am today.

I want to acknowledge my mother-in-law, Mrs. Shaila Raje, and my father-in-law, Mr. Manohar Raje, for their confidence in me and their continuous encouragement that is responsible for my success.

I would like to thank my beautiful wife, Swapna, for her unconditional love and unwavering support in all my endeavours and being my life partner sharing many precious moments with me. The encouragement that Swapna provides me is so powerful that I am able to achieve much more than I ever thought was possible for myself.

I want to thank my two impressive children, my daughter Sanjana and my son, Sahil, for being an inspiration to me and always being supportive and acting responsibly from very tender ages. Both of you amaze me with your intellectual capabilities and remember I do what I do, is always for you.

I want to acknowledge my sister, Mrs. Shilpa Dalvi, my brother in law, Mr. Hemant Dalvi and my talented nieces, Ms. Pranali Dalvi and Ms. Prachiti Dalvi, for always being there for me and offering unconditional support in every walk of life.

I want to acknowledge my coaches and mentors, Meir Ezra, Loral Langemeier, Bob Proctor, Jack Canfield, Robert Kiyosaki, Tony Robbins, and Brian Tracy, because of whom I developed the mindset and the courage to be a true entrepreneur. Through their powerful teachings and trainings, I am able to keep on achieving and exceeding my goals. I want to express my gratitude to all my friends and family that are always there for me and ready to lend a helping hand whenever I need one. Your willingness to contribute to my success and goals is quite commendable.

I want to acknowledge you the reader of my book for taking the time out from your schedule to make a difference in your life. I want to assure you that if you apply even some of the principles in this book, you will see a huge difference in your life and business. These are the exact principles that I use myself and have enormously helped my clients to achieve success.

Foreword

"Say YES and figure out how to get it done." This is an expression I use in my seminars, and the thoughts behind those words were quickly re-affirmed when speaking with the authors of, *Your Profound Success: 7 Powerful Ways to Skyrocket Your Business Using the Internet.* Amit Ambegaonkar and Raymond Aaron are two extremely successful entrepreneurs who have chosen to share their knowledge with you in very specific ways. Within these pages, you will find their experiences, secrets and helpful ideas for you to apply immediately.

Amit is a successful Wealth and Business Coach and an online entrepreneur. The strategies he teaches have already been proven to work on the internet. This book is about sharing his expertise with you to promote your business online and give you the visibility you need to acquire and nurture your clients.

Raymond brings his many years as an entrepreneur to the table and makes sure that Amit's message is simple, clear and down to earth. He stresses this so much that the first half of this book is about making sure you are ready to do business online. The second half of this book gives you all the basic tools that are required to actually go online with your business.

Loral Langemeier—Millionaire Maker

Loral Langemeier is a money expert, sought after speaker, entrepreneurial thought leader, and best-selling author of five books. She is on a relentless mission to change the conversation about money and empower people around the world to become millionaires.

About The Authors

Amit Ambegaonkar

Amit is a successful Wealth and Business Coach, who teaches how to gain financial freedom through various channels. Amit is an online entrepreneur, and the online strategies that he teaches have been proven to work on the Internet. He has the expertise to promote you business online, to give you the visibility you need to acquire and nurture your clients.

He really helps you to ease the complexity of the Internet world to make it easier for you to understand and apply.

Amit is a truly effective business coach, who understands the importance of having the right attitude and mindset. He believes in the integrations of right mindset and good ethics with proven business strategies to get the ultimate results in your life and business.

Raymond Aaron

Raymond is Canada's original Real Estate Guru, the creator of over 40 businesses and is a New York Times Bestselling Author. He has teamed up with Amit Ambegaonkar to help him leverage his brand with respect to Amit's expertise as an advisor and coach for building wealth using the internet.

Raymond has also helped countless others to achieve their dreams of financial success and to position themselves by writing books about their expertise. Some use these wonderful books as elaborate business cards or to position themselves as experts in their own fields or to increase the visibility of their brand. Raymond transforms lives by helping people tap into their own potential. Raymond also teaches via the many seminars he offers each year, through individual coaching and powerful workshops.

This brilliant man has devoted his life to helping others achieve the kind of wealth and lifestyle he enjoys himself. Raymond is a member of the International Who's Who of Entrepreneurs.

CHAPTER 1

The Entrepreneur Mindset

Your exciting journey begins here...

The mind is where everything originates. Have a look at everything around you. Everything that you see around you began as a thought in someone's mind. When the thought is acted upon with a lot of hard work and persistence, then you see the idea or the concept in existence.

If you think about every object that you see around you, you will realize the power of your mind.

Before we dive into the details of skyrocketing your business with the different online strategies, it is of paramount importance that you understand the concept and realize the importance of your mind.

Your mind is so powerful that it can help you achieve any goal that you give it.

As Napoleon Hill said, "Whatever your mind can conceive and believe, it can achieve."

However, the mind is also very dangerous, because if you start thinking about the negative things that might happen in your business, it can help you achieve those too. It is the Law of Attraction. It is an actual law like the law of gravity!

The best way to think about this is to look at the results that you have had in your life as of today. They are a result of your thinking and beliefs about yourself and your surroundings.

You might be wondering why I am talking about mindset and focus when you're supposed to be reading about online business strategies.

The reason I started with your mindset is that unless you have the correct mental framework it is challenging for you take your business to the next level. You are where you are today due to your thinking patterns and your beliefs.

Your mindset is the first place to start working, to bring about any change that you want.

In this book, we are going to talk about changing your mindset. So be on the lookout for tips in the book, as you read along!

The fact is that the more you understand the strategies in this book, the more you apply them, the more you can define your business, the more specific you can establish your goals and dreams, and the more success you are going to have.

The reason you may not have reached the level that you want in your business is that you do not have the above things clearly defined.

It may be the very reason why you have not been able to achieve what you want to achieve in your life.

You may think that the above statement is oversimplified, and I agree, it is. However, it is important that you start here and gradually get into the details of the concepts so that you will find it easier to apply them.

We are going to address the aspects that may be in your way of success, so that with the proper application of these principles, you can propel your business and your happiness in life to a whole different level.

So, are you ready?

What is mindset?

Your mindset can be defined as the set of attitudes held in your mind.

Mindset is a simple idea discovered by world-renowned Stanford University psychologist Carol Dweck, after decades of research on achievement and success—a simple idea that makes all the difference.

In a fixed mindset, people believe their basic qualities, like their intelligence or talent, are directly fixed traits. They spend their time documenting their intelligence or talent instead of developing them. They also believe that talent alone creates success – without effort. They're wrong!

In a growth mindset, people believe that their most basic abilities can be developed through dedication and hard work—brains and talent are just the starting point. This view creates a love of learning and resilience that is essential for great accomplishment. Virtually all great people have these qualities.

Teaching a growth mindset creates motivation and productivity in the worlds of business, education, and sports. It enhances relationships. When you read Mindset, you'll see how.

Mindsets are beliefs—beliefs about yourself and your most essential qualities. Think about your intelligence, your talents, your personality. Are these qualities simply fixed traits, carved in stone and that's that? Or are they things you can cultivate throughout your life?

People with a fixed mindset believe that their traits are just givens. They have a certain amount of brains and talent, and nothing can change that. If they have a lot, they're all set, but if they don't... So people in this mindset worry about their traits and how adequate they are. They have something to prove to themselves and others.

People with a growth mindset, on the other hand, see their qualities as things that can be developed through their dedication and effort. Sure they're happy if they're brainy or talented, but that's just the starting point. They understand that no one has ever accomplished great things—not Mozart, Darwin, or Michael Jordan—without years of passionate practice and learning.

http://mindsetonline.com/whatisit/themindsets/index.html

Do you have an employee or entrepreneur mindset?

Let us now dive into some of the differences between an entrepreneur mindset and an employee mindset. In doing so I don't mean to imply that one is better than the other. The reason I am trying to explain the difference between these two frameworks is because I want you to understand which context you fit in.

I have seen very successful businesses fail after they have reached some success, because their mindset was not developed to achieve the next level in their business.

I have seen that everyone has a combination of attributes, of an employee mindset and an entrepreneurial mindset. However, the ratio of employee thinking versus entrepreneurial thinking might vary from individual to individual.

Very few people have a 100% employee mind, and it would also be rare to find a person that has a 100% entrepreneurial mind.

In the case of the employee and the entrepreneur, the amount of work involved may differ depending on the position, the designation, and the responsibilities that the individual holds in their corporation or their own business.

It would be really hard to say who works harder. It would also be very hard to say who is usually more successful. There are employees who are successful and there are lots of entrepreneurs who are struggling, and vice versa.

The reason I wanted to make this clear is because success means different things for different people. If an employee is happy with his 9-to-5 job and is able to meet his obligations and enjoy his life, then that might be his definition of success.

On the other hand, there might be an entrepreneur who has been struggling for years and years and still unable to make ends meet and we're considering himself / herself unsuccessful.

Listed below are the features of an entrepreneur's mindset and an employee mindset.

The purpose of this book is to help entrepreneurs figure out the way to be successful in their business, and learn different ways to promote themselves to help their clients.

The reason I'm putting out this list of differentiation between an employee and an entrepreneurial mindset is that, if you have an employee mindset you need to change that to be a successful entrepreneur.

An employee mindset

1. You have a consistent schedule - for example from 9 AM to 5 PM 5 days a week.

2. You get paid for your work on an hourly or salary basis. There may be some bonuses along the way. The pay will come on a regular basis, and is not subject to your performance in many cases.

3. You will be eligible to get paid vacation and paid time off.

4. You will have a boss who is over-demanding, and pressures you to meet deadlines and achieve certain goals.

5. You may have very good health and dental insurance coverage through your workplace. You enjoy this feature of your

organization and even may think of changing your employer based on the benefits received.

6. Your company may contribute to your retirement savings plans, or may match your contribution to some retirement accounts. You may have already planned out your path of retirement and do not wish to change that.

7. You may get additional discounts from your company for the events outside of your company, as well as some general discounts from stores or membership sites.

8. You hate to be outside of your comfort zone. Over the period of months and years of service with a company, you develop a sense of comfort with the corporation. Working for another company or organization, or even working with the same company in a different role becomes more and more challenging.

9. You are not comfortable with taking risks and chances. You have a certain level of comfort and security that you have established working for a company as an employee. Just the idea of going into business for yourself seems too overwhelming for you, and you only tend to see the huge challenges, difficulties, and obstacles that come with starting your own business.

Your Profound Success

10. Nobody in your family has either tried to be in business, or they may have failed when they started their business.

The other possibility is that you know someone, either a friend or relative, that had started a business and failed, thus leaving him or her in a financial and emotional turmoil.

An entrepreneur mindset

The mindset of an entrepreneur differs from an employee mindset. Here are some differences:

1. **You understand that you're paid only on your performance.**

   If you try to do business with an employee mindset, you will not succeed. You have to let go of the concept of getting paid directly for the work that you do. In other words, it may happen that you have invested a significant amount of money and time in a business project or a business idea, and have no returns or positive cash flow for some time – maybe months or maybe even years. As long as you have planned out how you are going to pay the expenses of your business and yourself, you are okay.

2. **Thinking outside the box.**

   In an employee structure, you are given a job you are expected to do it every day. An entrepreneur, on the other hand, always needs to think outside the box. An entrepreneur has to think about the

11

short term as well as the long term. Entrepreneurs have to think creatively about various challenging situations and how to overcome them.

3. As an entrepreneur, you are committing yourself to lifetime learning. You should be willing to learn from your mistakes, and also other people's mistakes, as this will drastically reduce the time you will take to achieve your success.

4. As an entrepreneur, you do not get any paid vacation, sick leave or holidays. You do not have the sense of security as with a regular 9-to-5 job.

Having a business mindset is very crucial to achieving success in your business. In fact, it is impossible to achieve success in your business if you have an employee mindset.

I know a lot of coaches and mentors that focus their attention on training their students to have an amazing mindset so that they can have an exponential growth in their business.

When I started my businesses, I had to study, understand and adapt to this entrepreneurial mindset.

I will tell you that it is not as easy as it looks, because as an employee you can see a paycheck every 2 weeks or once per month, whereas with the business model, you are lucky if you make some money even at the end of 3 months!

I did not always have an entrepreneurial mindset. I had to train myself to get into that.

I grew up in a family where no one had achieved true success in business. My father worked for a big multinational company. On his retirement, he was awarded a wristwatch and a bouquet of flowers as a token of appreciation for 40 years of work!

From that moment onwards, I've always been shocked to see the token of appreciation that people receive for working for a company for years and years.

One employee told me that he received a $200 jacket for working for a company for 40 years! Another employee said that she received three days paid leave as her gift for 45 years of hard work!

The surprising part of this is that people who receive these tokens of appreciation seem to be very happy about receiving them at the end of their career. When I look at these tokens of appreciation, I truly feel that these are nowhere near the value of the contribution that these dedicated and hard-working individuals gave to these corporations. I strongly believe that the work that they did for these corporations should have been appreciated more often, and also that they should have been rewarded much better at the end of their career.

I am sure you also may have some examples where you have seen how small, petty, or insignificant these gifts and rewards are, compared to the dedication, hard work and sincerity the employee has shown towards the corporation.

When I came across these examples, the decision for me to get into my own business was pretty straightforward.

The Power of YOUR mind

Starting with the right mindset is very critical, as this will determine how well you do in your business. Your mind is the ultimate controller of your destiny and how much you will achieve in life.

To demonstrate the importance of the effect that a human mind can have on the body, look at a person with multiple personality disorder, also known as dissociative identity disorder.

The fascinating thing about these people is the amount of change that takes place in their bodies when their personality changes. It's interesting to note that not only are there talking and behavior changes, but there are also a lot of physical changes that take place.

For example, there are changes in vision, illnesses and diseases, insulin levels, burn marks and scars. Their beliefs, their gender association, even x-rays and CT scans change when they change their personalities. This simply goes to show you that the way you think cannot just make a difference emotionally, but also has the power to change your body.

Our mind has two components: the conscious and the subconscious. It is said that about 90% of our behavior happens off the subconscious level.

The conscious mind controls everything that we do at the conscious level, but a huge part of our day is actually automatic. The subconscious mind is the reason and the force behind getting things done.

Do you ever drive to work and reach your destination, but do not remember the exact route that you took? What signals you got green? What intersections had traffic?

My point is that all of this daily driving is where your subconscious mind takes over.

Bob Proctor, an award-winning author and a world famous life coach, emphasizes the importance of the subconscious mind. According to Bob Proctor, the subconscious mind is the mind where is all the thoughts are compared, studied and applied.

We act totally according to our subconscious programming, which he calls paradigms.

Some of these beliefs may be so deeply rooted in our minds that to believe otherwise seems almost impossible. We have to undergo a huge amount of training and learning to make any significant changes to our paradigms.

Hence, thinking of success and focusing on it is critical, as the mind then works to find success in everything that we are doing. If you train your brain correctly, it can come up with answers to some of the most complicated questions. Let us look at a very common example. When I bought my first car – a gold Toyota Corolla, I started to see gold Toyota Corollas everywhere! Before that time I'm pretty sure there must have been gold Toyota Corollas all over the city; however, I seem to have missed them!

Now that we understand this principle of mind, we realize that our mind sees the opportunities that we challenge it mind with.

It is therefore very critical that you keep your focus on the successes that you want to achieve in your life and in your business, so that you keep seeing the opportunities to make you successful.

Use your mind to your advantage

I have personally used the power of my mind to overcome a lot of physical ailments and heal my body, and I continue to do so on a regular basis!

I want to point out that this does not mean you have to be positive 100% of the time. Even the most positive and successful people that I know have their phases when they dip into to the pool of negativity.

However, the distinction between successful people and unsuccessful people is the amount of time they spend being depressed or in the negative state.

A successful positive person may go to this phase of negativity but springs out of it almost instantaneously, or in far less time than others!

One of the most efficient techniques that I have learned to change the state of your mind towards positivity is from Tony Robbins and is as follows:

Change of body position: if you're sitting in one place looking down and thinking about some depressing, negative thoughts it's tough to just perk up yourself in that position.

But imagine what would happen if you stand and start jumping and smiling to yourself with the widest smile you've ever had? Or start running as fast as you can, or doing some high thrust activity.

I can assure you that if you can do that it will be impossible for you to remain in the depressed state. Research has proven that just a couple of minutes of a change in body position can induce a change in your mental state.

Now that you are clear about having a right mainframe and understand the power of your mind to get you the result that you want, let's move to the next exciting step!

CHAPTER 2

Why are you here?

Do you know your Driver?

Just think about the most successful people on this planet and really try to analyze why they became so successful.

Think about people like Steve Jobs, Bill Gates, Michael Dell, Mark Zuckerberg, Jack Canfield, Elon Musk, Tiger Woods, Ben Johnson, etc. If we tried to analyze their success stories to find out how they could reach the levels of success that any average person cannot even think about, what is the answer?

I have personally read, studied and discussed a lot of these successful individuals and I have come to realization that there is one common thread that ties them all together.

To achieve that level of success requires hard work, vision and dedication. But although all these things are very important and cannot be ignored, I believe that the most important driver for them was their PASSION.

Passion is the strong and barely controllable emotion.

Passion is a very strong feeling about a person or a thing. Passion is an intense emotion, a compelling enthusiasm or desire for something.

The reason this is a great starting point to start your business is because it is going to give you the greatest leverage in anything that you do in your business. Doing something that you love is the ultimate motivator. A confused mind does not do anything.

It would be great for you to know that your business will go through a lot of ups and downs, and it's your passion that's going to pick you up each and every time you fall.

You may already be aware that there are going to be some roadblocks, some challenges, and some difficulties before you encounter any kind of success in your business. I am giving you the force that's going to keep you going through all these challenges.

If you are able to discover your passion, define it in detail, understand what it is and actually see it happening, it will be so much easier for you not only to succeed in your business but also to reach new heights.

If you are unable to determine what your real passion is, then I would recommend you read an amazing book called, 'The Passion Test" by Janet Attwood.

'The Passion Test" outlines a clear way to determine your passion. Once you master the technique in that book, it will take you about 15 minutes to figure out what your passion is. I take the passion test myself every 3 months, and get amazing new energy to work at my business and my personal life!

In the meantime, to get you started on discovering your passion or to find out if your passion is well defined and on track, please answer the following questions:

- What is it that you really love to do?

- Can you keep it simple and straightforward?

- Does it get you really excited?

- What is your theme – sports, entertainment, business, travel, etc?

- Can you talk about it for the next 10 minutes without any hesitation or preparation?

- What problems do you love to solve for others?

- What makes you really happy?

- When do you feel really special and appreciated?

- Where do you go when you visit a bookstore?

- What products and services really excite you?

When you are trying to figure out your passion, the more options on a list that you can come up with, the better. Then you can really start to focus on the one thing that excites you the most.

Once you are able to figure this out, write it down on a clean piece of paper and read it out loud. Even as you go through this experience you should be getting a feeling of immense pleasure and satisfaction.

Congratulations!!! You have just done something that ONLY 3% of the entire population does!!!

Please write out your passion in BOLD CAPITAL letters right here:

_____

_____

_____

What drives you to excellence?

The majority of the people study, get into a job or a business, start their work in that, work very hard, make some money, support their family with that income, have fun within their means, and then retire.

This is truly the life cycle of the majority of the people around us. I believe that they miss a very important component that they should consider earlier in their life; and actually base their life on it.

Wouldn't you agree that if you were working on something that you really love and care for, you would be able to get maximum results?

Wouldn't you agree that if you can focus on things that appeal to you that you agree with you would be able to give your best?

If it is so easy to just do what you love, to follow your passion, and to focus on things that you like, why do we see so many people struggling?

I believe that the simple answer is that they have never given serious thought about how and what they could achieve in life, about what they should focus on in life. They have also never developed the mindset that they could WIN.

It goes back to our early childhood programming that our parents, friends, relatives inscribed in our minds without they being conscious about it and that decides our future today

As a child, we go through a lot of 'do not do this', 'do not do that'. Maybe the person meant it at that particular time and in that particular instance. But because, until the age of seven, our subconscious mind is wide open to suggestions and commands, and accepts everything without questioning, these are taken as facts and ingrained in our minds as rules.

Now even after so many years, we have these rules that we abide by, and that determine how we live our life.

To illustrate this fact, Jack Canfield gives us an amazing example. When a baby elephant is born, the elephant's leg is tied to a small wooden post so that he does not run away. When the baby tries to break away, it is impossible for the baby to break the rope. There are a number of times that the baby tries to do so, and over a period of time it learns that it cannot break the rope.

Years later, the elephant grows into this gigantic animal that weighs 5 tons and can easily break that tied rope, but it remains within the constraints of the rope.

As a baby it has learnt that it cannot break that tie, so as an adult, it does not even try!!! Yes, the elephant doesn't even try! WOW!!

Takeaway: Do you have anything tying you back as an adult?

Defining your purpose

Purpose is defined as the reason for which something is done or created, or for which something exists.

WHY ARE YOU HERE?

In one of my coaching sessions with Mr. Raymond Aaron, he asked me this question, and I couldn't believe that I did not have an answer for him.

Once I was able to answer that question for myself, the clarity that I got in my life was so profound that I really started moving in the right direction.

What a dynamic impact this question had on my life! It had such a profound impact on my business and my family life, so I want you to benefit from this question, the same way as I did. I therefore want you to take the upcoming challenge very seriously.

Today, I challenge you to answer this question: WHY ARE YOU HERE?

Yes, I want you to really dig down deep and find out your why. Believe me, this why is the one that's going to keep you going when the times get tough. All the successful people I know have such a strong why that nobody can deter them from their goals.

To help you out in understanding this further, I am offering you the help you need to figure it out.

I would like you to come up with your answer for this question and email your answer to me. I will personally respond to your email. I want to see your commitment, your dedication and your compliance to your success. So please send me an email with "Why am I here" in the subject line and send the email to Amit@YourProfound Solutions.com.

I understand that this is a very heavy loaded question and you may need some time to think over it, and even consult your mentor or your coach about it. Let me tell you that if you can figure this out, the rest of the book is going to be so easy for you to follow.

ARE YOU GETTING THE PICTURE?

Throughout this book, I know you might be looking for a giant secret, a hidden formula or an untold story, an 'aha' moment, that will change your business or your life, but here I am telling you straight off the bat that there is no such thing in this book.

The matter-of-fact is you are going to find lots of small nuggets to apply in your life and your business today. And your success is going to show up as the sum total of all the small nuggets applied in your life and business.

I want to also emphasize that this book is a practical application book. Whatever we have discussed so far in the book I would highly encourage you to apply, for you to get astounding results.

There might be things that you miss, so I encourage you to come back to these chapters and read them again to make sure that you have gotten every piece of information and are able to use it for your benefit.

The only limits in our life are those we impose on ourselves.

- Bob Proctor

Passion and Purpose

Now that you know about passion and purpose, how do these two powerful concepts come together?

I appreciate you following along and also doing all the exercises along the way. This will really help you identifying and understanding your passion and your purpose.

Now we have to put these together to get the most amazing formula for your life and your business.

Following your passion is very important. Passion is the fuel that gets you going. Passion is what starts the engine. But passion isn't everything.

To achieve the most remarkable success it is crucial that you have your passion and your purpose aligned with each other. Your ultimate goal should be to meet your life purpose as your follow your passion.

So what is the difference between passion and purpose?

Passion is your compelling emotions behind your dreams. Your feelings drive your passion. Purpose is the *why* behind it all. Purpose is the deep reason for your existence. Purpose is what gets you up in the morning.

In other words, if you find yourself not motivated enough or not following through with what you are promising yourself, you have not figured out your passion and your purpose.

Now that the concept of purpose and passion is clear, let us move to the next core value for your success...The genius in YOU.

Discover your genius

Yes you have one. Believe me. And that's the reason I have said *discover* your genius; you don't have to *find* your genius. What can you do that very few people can do?

Your genius is already there. It's in you and it is a matter of going deep into your mind and discovering what is your true genius.

The sooner you are able to discover it and the sooner you start implementing the strategies, the more the successful you will be. Do not wait until you figure out all the things and then start. Start applying your genius, and all other things will start falling into place.

I am sometimes shocked that people go through their entire lives without even realizing what their genius is. Sometimes they do realize their true genius but they discount it and shake it off, thinking that is not a big deal, and so they choose to ignore it instead of focusing on it.

I was associated with a lot of people who were in their 80s and 90s. It was very interesting for me to see that these people have gone through their lives without realizing their genius.

During my conversations with them, when I brought up something that they were really good at, they would be very prompt in discounting that fact and not accepting my compliment. They sometimes even gave me a counterstatement to let me know why it was not true. WOW!

Just think of it: 80 – 90 years of paradigms and beliefs about something.

So do you think that if you have a paradigm that is about 20 or 30 years old you can change it more easily?

Of course I realize that after programming their subconscious mind for so many years it might not be easy for them. The paradigms that they have in their minds must be so strong that to change them at this point in time would not be easy.

Beliefs can be impacted by repetition or reinforcements. Or something that happens that is so impactful that your belief can change in a moment! For example, if a person learns some brutal facts about smoking or experiences a close friend's death due to smoking, may give up smoking that same day.

Do not let these beliefs about yourself drag you down from achieving more in life. Don't let these be the limiting factors in your mind for your progress. Do not let these self-limiting factors be the ceiling that you must succumb to.

You demonstrate unique mastery over something. I would encourage you to discover your genius and work on it to enhance it, empower it, and align it with your purpose and your passion.

The Rocking Chair Test

THE ROCKING CHAIR EXERCISE

Let's put our thinking caps on. Start to imagine that you are in your 80s and you are sitting in a quiet place. Imagine it is a place where you love to sit quietly and meditate. Imagine it's a place where you find tranquility. Imagine a place that is away from home, where you feel at peace.

Now imagine that you are sitting on the rocking chair and reflecting back on your life. You are thinking about what you've achieved in your life, what the goals you've achieved in your life, how you have developed yourself, and how successful have you become in your life.

Also try to think about some of the things that you did not achieve in your life. What are the opportunities that you could have taken and did not; what are the things that you could have done but did not; was there anything in your youth that you could have done better; is there anything in your life that you wish you would have done more or less of? If you take this exercise really seriously and do it with your full concentration, it may lead you to things that your conscious mind may not be able to explain. If you go into the times of the period mentioned in the exercise, of thinking they you're really looking back and thinking about the goals that you wanted to achieve, the goals that you should have achieved, and the goals that you didn't achieve, it may give you the direction that you want to go as of today.

This rocking chair experiment has helped thousands of people focus their energy, their goals and their life.

Take Action NOW!

I am sure you must have read a lot of books. I do not want this to be just one more book that you have just read. So please take action. This book that you're reading is really not a fiction book; this book is an action book. So if you go through this entire book just as reading material that's fine; you will enjoy it and I'm sure you'll take some nuggets. But if you really want to progress in your life, if you want to achieve greater success, then I would strongly encourage you to stop reading this book and apply the valuable lesson that you've just learned. Apply the concept that you're learning in the book before you move on to the next step.

In life, we find we are more disappointed by the things we didn't do than the ones we did. So if you are feeling regret as an imaginary 80 year old, take it to heart. Use this tool as a shot of courage to go for something you really want.
Take Action Now!

CHAPTER 3

Where Are You Going?

The Excitement Begins...

Now we come to the exciting part of your journey in finding out where you want to go. We now get a little creative and start to think, imagine and dream about the things that you really want in life. Now I know that some things may not be easy for you to figure out. But believe me, the 'how' is not relevant right now. Just follow your instincts and put it down on paper.

Please note that I am not asking you to think how you are going to get there. The intent of this exercise is to get on paper whatever your mind can think of that it wants to achieve and experience. What do you want to do, experience, have or feel in your lifetime? What are the things that you will want to possess and would love to have at your disposal?

Building this list sounds easy, but it may be very difficult for some of us to do. The reason is that when we talk about dreaming we only think about the dreams that we get while we're sleeping. However, the real dreams are actually those that do not let us sleep!

So I would encourage you to write down 100 things that you really want to achieve in your life before you die. Yes, the correct number is

100. When you start, this might seem like a huge number and you may stop at 10 or 12; but please keep going and list 100 things you want to do or have in your lifetime. This is exactly what top achievers have done to become successful. All we are doing is following their footsteps so we can reach where they have reached.

Many great achievers and successful people have put their hundred things on paper and started to work on them one by one. Some of these dreams may be materialistic, some may be more emotional; some may be related to travel, some may be related to doing charities, and that's all fine and great. It's your list and it should be as unique as you are!

Once you have this list of 100 dreams, or things that you want to do before you die, you're ready to begin to achieve them one by one!

Question: What if I can only put down 10 dreams?
Answer: That's a great question!

If you would like the best results in your life I would really encourage you to follow the exact method that I have listed in this book so that you get success beyond measure. However, if you are having trouble achieving a step, I do not want you to stop at that step and not go further. Give it your best shot to go from 10 to at least 40 or 50 and then proceed to the next step.

Knowing where you are and where you are headed

In his book, *The Seat of the Soul,* Gary Zukav says, "When we align our thoughts, emotions, and actions with the highest part of ourselves, we are filled with enthusiasm, purpose and meaning. When the personality comes fully to serve the energy of its soul, that is authentic empowerment."

To me, this chapter is one of the most important chapters in this entire book.

The importance of this chapter is so high because this is really where your journey begins. This is the foundation that we are going to form and develop over time as your journey with me evolves further.

It does not matter how life has treated you until today or until this moment. However, it does matter how you will treat your life from this moment onwards!

In 2009, I was at the stage of my life when I was considering lot of businesses that were online, off-line, professional, and franchises. I looked and considered businesses that involved solo entrepreneurs and working in teams, having a small company and employing staff models, etc. It all seemed too confusing and overwhelming. I knew there must be an easier way to do this!

That is the time when I got involved in coaching myself and getting tremendous insights about how to manage my life.

I realized that the aspect of 'knowing where I am and where I want to go' is so foundational to everything that I must do.

I immediate planned out in detail, what I wanted to do, and that's exactly when things started shaping up for me! This alignment with my goals and purpose was the critical component that I was missing. I therefore want to emphasize the importance of this step, so that you do not work too hard in a business that you did not truly want to do.

Let us start by examining exactly where you are today. The following table will help you to identify where you stand today with respect to different aspects of your life.

Please note that some of these aspects are not directly related to your business. However, as we are starting out, we want to look at life as a whole.

You can also find a soft copy of this same table online on www.yourprofoundsuccess.com/whereyouaretoday

WHERE YOU ARE TODAY:

DATE:

NUMBER OF PEOPLE IN DATABASE	
NUMBER OF ACTIVE CLIENTS	
NUMBER OF TOTAL CLIENTS	
AVERAGE $ SALE PER CLIENT	
MONTHLY PROFIT LAST MONTH	
TOTAL $ IN RETIREMENT ACCOUNTS	
TOTAL NET WORTH TODAY	

People are busy... going fast... really fast, somewhere.

A lot of people that we talk to tell us they are *busy*. The majority of people do not even have 10 to 15 minutes to set aside for the task if something comes up. Being busy actually gives them a sensation that they are important. By being busy they think they're getting a lot of things done and hence are being very efficient in their work.

A lot of people may just be busy managing their day-to-day life and their day-to-day business. If you ask them at the end of the day what they achieved, they really would not have a concrete answer for you.

I sometimes wonder how many people, who are really busy throughout the day for months and years together, really take the time to actually plan their life. How many of them actually think about the goals they want to achieve? How many of them have a life purpose and passion that is defined?

These are the 97% of the people! You are now amongst the 3% of the people that are successful and on your way to achieve some phenomenal success!! Congratulations!

Constantly working and trying to do more

The people that we meet on a day-to-day basis, that are always busy, are not necessarily busy because they're working too hard. They may be working inefficiently and therefore may be busier than they should be.

Maybe they did not have their priorities lined up in sequence to make themselves be more efficient.

One of the greatest techniques of successful people is not that they do more, but that they prioritize. An average person might put the same amount of effort in all the tasks, no matter how important they are.

On the other hand, the successful person will work really hard on the aspect of business that he gives top priority to, and also what he does the best.

This is probably the most important aspect that distinguishes the successful people from the not so successful people. The term that they might use is called 'leverage.'

The richest person in the world and the poorest person in the world both have exactly 24 hours in a day. It is what they do with those 24 hours that determines where they go in life.

Get, Set, GOAL...

> *If you know what to do to reach your goal,*
> *it's not a big enough goal.*
> Bob Proctor

Goals are such a crucial part of the entire business plan that I have given this the maximum weight for success of any individual and business.

Some of the aspects about goal setting are simple, but you would be surprised and somewhat shocked to see how many people actually follow through at this step.

Do you know why 90% of people do not achieve their goals?

When I learned about the answer to this question, I could not believe it. I actually expected the answer to be a very complex and intricate answer that would give me a lot of insight into how I could achieve my own goals.

However, to my amazement, and probably yours too, the reason why 90% of people do not achieve their goals is that they do not set them up!!!

> *If what you are doing is not moving you towards your goals,*
> *then it's moving you away from your goals.*
> Brian Tracy

The system that I follow is one of the most recognized systems, and proven to work for hundreds and hundreds of people around the world.

It is a system that has such a systematic approach that anyone at any time can ask you how you are doing with your goals for the month, and you will have an exact answer ready to give them!

This successful system has been designed and founded by Raymond Aaron. In the system Raymond has a form that enlists six key areas in which goals need to be set.

At the beginning of the month, sit down with a pen and paper and write down these 6 main areas that you want to achieve your goals in.

This is the MAINLY (R) SYSTEM by Raymond Aaron:

- MESS: this is a circumstance in which what is outside of you is not equal to what is inside of you. Any situation, physical thing, relationship, any aspect of your environment, or anything that you are tolerating or is not working, is a mess.

- ACKNOWLEDGEMENT: this is the way to show your appreciation to a person, a company or to group of people.

- INCOME: This is a way to increase your income or decrease your expenses; this is where you record your money goals.

- NEW OPPORTUNITIES: This is something new that you want to have or do, that you have not had or done before. It might be within real estate or not. It is a new way of doing something in your life or some new expedience.

- LEARN: this is something you want to learn in order to help you in your business or personal life.

- YOURSELF: This is doing something just for yourself; taking care of you. Think of what you would just love to allow yourself to do, or to allow yourself as a treat.

This method of goal setting and scoring your goals gives exact information about how you are progressing.

I highly recommend reading Raymond Aaron's book – *Double Your Income Doing What You Love.*

Here are some rules for setting up your goals:

- Very simple to understand.
- Very specific.
- Stated always in the positive.
- Has a clear action outlined.
- Has a definite date of completion of goal.
- In alignment with your purpose and passion.

Setting a goal is the first step in turning the invisible into the visible.
Tony Robbins

How do you know you have achieved them?

The method that you use for setting your goals has to be very clear, simple and easy to understand. Anyone should be able to look at your goal sheet at the end of the month and know exactly how you have done that month.

Your goal recording system should be very clear, and should be geared towards the results that you want to achieve. For example, having a goal of losing some weight in the next 90 days is not effective.

Instead of that, if you have a goal of weighing 160 pounds on March 31, 2017 it becomes a specific and clear goal.

If you do this for all six areas listed above at the end of each month, it will be very easy for you look at the sheet and tell yourself exactly how you have done for that month.

This is truly one of the best ways to recognize record and the progress with all your goals.

Once you develop the habit of writing your goals and scoring them, you get an immense boost to keep writing them each and every month. This acts as your focused to-do list!

Jack Canfield, who is also a master teacher in goal setting, also emphasizes the importance of goal setting and his 7th principle in his book – *The Success Principles,* in which he talks about unleashing the power of goal setting.

Jack Canfield recommends setting goals in 7 different categories, with dates for each of the goals and the reason why you want that goal achieved, or how would you feel once that goal is achieved.

- Financial Goals: income, savings, investments, debt reduction and credit.

  E.g.: a. By Dec 31, 2018, I will be earning $10,000 a month pre-tax income.

- Career/ Business Goals: New Job, Self-employed, Sales volume

  E.g. I will start my own restaurant consulting business by September 18, 2017.

- Free time/ Family Time: days off, hobbies, Special Events.

  E.g. Starting 1 Feb, 2016 I will take off 3 weeks in May and 3 weeks in October.

- Health and Appearance Goals: Lose weight, feel younger, eat better.

  E.g. I will be at my ideal weight of 170 lbs by November 1, 2017.

- Relationship Goals: family, mentors, business alliances, staff

  E.g. I will re-establish communication with my brother by December 1, 2016.

- Personal Growth: education, spiritual growth, therapy and training.

  E.g. I will attend the 15 August, 2016 training on negotiating skills.

- Making a difference: charitable giving, church tithes, mentoring
  E.g. I will volunteer mentor at least one young entrepreneur
  starting Fall 2017.

So, to know if your goal has been achieved is dependent on the way you set it up. If you set up a goal that is clearly defined, it is much easier to understand, and even easier to decide if you have accomplished it.

Set a goal to achieve something that is so big, so exhilarating, that it excites you and scares you at the same time.
Bob Proctor

Get Help Now!!

Do you ever clean your house before you call your cleaning lady?
Do you manually wash your car before taking it to an automated car wash?

NO, right? It would almost seem funny to do that.

You are right. Then why do so many people think like that when it comes to taking the help of a mentor or a coach? People think that they will take a coach when they earn some money in their business. They think they will hire a coach after they achieve at least some success in their business!

Isn't that a little backward thinking?

Wouldn't you want the help of your coach or mentor before you start to work hard in your business, to get guidance if you are headed in the right direction?

Wouldn't you love the fact that you will get proper direction and focus if you talk to your coach or mentor before you start working on your major goals/dreams?

Get a coach and/or mentor

With my association with top leaders, mentors, coaches, high performing colleagues and successful entrepreneurs, if you ask me what is the one thing that all these people have in common, my answer would be that they have mentors!

Can you think of three to five people that are in this category?

Now can you think of three to five people who, according to you, have achieved great success?

I can almost guarantee that the people that are successful have had some coach or mentor to get them there. The one thing that is common in all these successful entrepreneurs, beyond any doubt, is that a great mentor or a great coach has trained them.

Have you seen any Olympic medal winner without a coach? Have you seen any successful sportsman without a coach? Have you seen a businessman who has reached the top of his business without being guided mentored or coached by a successful businessman? Let me tell you honestly that if there is any one thing that is common in all these successful people is that they have a mentor.

So, what about you? Do you have a mentor? Do you have a coach? Do you have somebody you can ask for help when you get stuck? Do you have somebody that you can email, text or call and get some help in an effort to overcome the obstacles that you're facing in your business and your life?

If you don't have such a person now is the time to get one.

The most common objections that I hear are: Where do I find them? They must be expensive. I don't have the money. I agree these are all very valid and genuine objections. I'm not going to discount them at all. The reason for that is I myself was in that scenario and I have gone through the difficulty of not knowing where to look for good mentors and coaches, and also where to get the money to be coached.

Let me help you by asking you to just start looking around. Yes! If you are thinking of opening a restaurant of your own, what if you go to the owner of the best restaurant in the city and ask him for about half an hour to meet for coffee? Why don't you meet him and pick his brain about what he did to be successful?

Now that you may be feeling more organized, at least in your mind, it's time to take the next step!

I would emphasize that to get the maximum benefit from this book, it is recommended that you work in this specific order. This order has been proven and tested to work!

If you need any help figuring out your path to success, feel free to contact me at Amit@YourProfoundSolutions.com

CHAPTER 4

Laying the Foundation of Your Business

An Inside look at your Business

I have met so many entrepreneurs that are working hard in their business, but their income is not even near to their potential. Their income, their status, and their visibility are not where they should be at all. If you are such an entrepreneur, you will relate to this.

You may be in a situation that you feel you have so much knowledge and expertise; you have so much value that you can give but have no one asking for it. You want to share your experience but people around you do not know about your power and wisdom.

If that is you, you may want to have a look at your business model and the channels that you use to promote yourself and your products or services.

If you are working too hard and making less money, your business model may be the factor that is preventing you from experiencing exponential growth.

The fact of the matter is we have never received any business education. In schools there are hardly any subjects that covered the aspect of business as it happens in your life.

It is therefore crucial that when we enter the business world, we are exposed to so many different aspects and avenues that we have to deal with solo entrepreneurs.

Some of the technical aspects of the business need to be taken care of, with the help of your accountant and your lawyer. They will be in a position to advise you about registering your business as a corporation, or to continue in your own name.

After that comes deciding the name of your business, its structure, its location, your business logo, your business cards, your business slogan etc.

For all these aspects of the business to fall into place may take some time, depending on the experience that you have and also the professionals that you hire.

Some of the other aspects of the business that need your careful consideration are as follows:

- How much time can you devote to your business?
- Do you do it full-time or part-time?
- What is your monetary investment in the business?
- Will you have any partners working with you in the business?
- Do you plan to have any employees?
- What is your ongoing monthly business budget?

- Do you have an exit plan for your business?
- How do you plan to do your accounting?
- How do you plan to do your marketing?
- Who will be handling the sales?
- What will be the method of delivery of all your products and services?

If you don't have a business right now

If you do not have a business right now it may not be such a bad thing. Let me explain.

If you do not have a business, this is a great time to study and compare different business models, different business ideas, and different business structures. Consider what works best for you.

A lot of entrepreneurs fail to do this step, and when they are right in the middle of the business they try to think of these things.

If you decide to look up businesses online be very careful as to what you opt for. There are a variety of businesses online that are scams. You really need to do a lot of homework before getting into any company.

I have association with two of the most of the reputed companies online, and they have a tremendous reputation for being authentic and real. If you do not have any idea of what business to get into, I would be able to guide you to get into a very profitable business that can be automated.

You may also find a lot of multilevel marketing companies trying to recruit you in today's businesses. If you know the company well and have used their products and are happy with them, do not worry about trying them out.

If you're having trouble finding the most authentic companies online then just send me an email and I will let you know my personal preferences about the companies that I recommend to my clients. Please contact me at my email address Amit@YourProfound Solutions.com

Another way to make money online is with something called affiliate marketing. With affiliate marketing, you do not have to come up with any of your own products. There are some well-known companies that only require you to send your contacts, your clients, or your database, to their website. You will collect commissions on any sale happening through the traffic that you send to their main website.

Affiliate marketing is really a win-win concept, because you as an entrepreneur do not have to come up with any product, you do not have to do any research, and you are not responsible for any delivery, shipping or handling of the product.

Kinds of businesses

There are two kinds of businesses that you could be involved in. One is called a service-based business, where you offer your services to your clients. Examples are a real estate agent, a coach, or a physiotherapist.

You may be involved in a product-based business. In a product-based business the products are the focal point of your business. Example: KFC, McDonald's, etc.

If you're in a position where you're deciding what business to get into, it is usually a good idea to get into a service-based business. The reason I'm saying that is because in a product-based businesses you are really selling the product itself, which has to be better than any competition out there for you to get the sale. Whereas in a service-based business you can specialize in one specific niche market that you are an expert in, and be really successful.

Test your products – if you decide to go into a product-based business it is crucial that you use the products yourself and have an honest opinion about these products that they are the best products! If you believe that the products have some flaw in them and that they are not good for the client that you are talking to, you will not be very successful in your business. Also do thorough research on the product that you're about to promote. This product that you're promoting may be your own product or you might be acting as an affiliate to sell someone else's product. Please bear in mind that your future potential customers and anyone that you share your business with is going to associate you to the product. I cannot emphasize the importance of this particular feature and how much significance it has, not just for this business but also for any future businesses that you might undertake.

Survey the market for demand:

A lot of businesses big and small use this feature before they launch a product or a business. Through existing channels and marketing methods, corporations and companies hand over surveys to be done by customers in order to figure out if their business would run well in that specific market.

Along with this, you also need to decide whether you are a business-to-business or business-to-consumer business.

Once you have decided your business model I would strongly encourage you to discuss it with your coach or mentor. Your coach should have been selected by you and have the expertise. It would be ideal if your coach has he reached that specific level that you want to achieve. I have personally spent a lot of money, time and energy to learn about business that I want to be successful at through my coaches and experts. Now thinking about this, I realize that I definitely would not have been able to do without my coaches and mentors. If you don't have a mentor, I cannot stress the importance of having a mentor.

How to structure for success

The MISSING INGREDIENT:

In my experience being an entrepreneur and helping lots of other entrepreneurs, Entrepreneurs share a common characteristic of having many great ideas and wanting to do so many things at the same time.

You cannot take off with two planes at a time! Though this is funny, it makes its point. If you are trying to achieve two major goals at the same time, you are trying to take off with two planes at the same time.

In my earlier chapters, we have already established the best way to prosper in your businesses is to focus on your purpose and your passions. The main reason that you may not be successful is that you are targeting too many areas to master! So the underlying message for this section is to FOCUS!!

Because our businesses have so many moving parts, there are many aspects that need to be dealt with to make our business successful. We have several aspects to take care of before our business really starts booming.

If you think about all the things on your to-do list, how long do you think you are going to take to complete each and every task on your list? Probably forever right?

On your to-do list you still have about 30 to 40 things that need to be done in the next two weeks. Am I right?

That is exactly the reason for this section. You need to prioritize and focus your attention on the most important aspect.

Do you feel overwhelmed by all these things that are to be done? If you are like majority of the entrepreneurs, your answer will be yes.

Even if you take into account one business that already has a niche, which has a target audience and a niche market, there are still lots of moving parts that need to be addressed in order for that business to progress.

Why am I saying all this?

If you are an entrepreneur, you will relate to me in a lot of these aspects that I just talked about.

Now, let us go one step further. Now that you have so many things on your agenda to do, and you have a fantastic dream and the goals that you want to achieve, let's take the next step!

The Foundation of your Business:

Here is an excellent list for you to get started on understanding your power, and the strength and value of your business:

1. Identify the core values in the business

What does your company really believe in? What is it that your business can thrive on? What are the qualities that your business will not give away, even for a million dollars? Some examples of this may be – honesty, integrity, timeliness, delivery of product, quality, precision, excel at customer services, refund policies well-defined, etc.

The more clear you are in defining and identifying the core values of your business, the more customers will relate to you. This is because customers always value the company that does exactly what it says it will do.

For example, if your dignity is one of your highest core values, any promise you make the customer will be fulfilled, and this will cause the customer to develop loyalty towards your company and your brand.

2. Selecting your Niche

Because your business is based on your calling and your purpose, you excel at your business! You are the master at what you do.

Here is the most important point – It does not have to be vast and wide.

For example –real estate agents do not have to master all the types of real estate transactions that take place. The real estate agent can very well say "I am an expert at selling high rise condos in the downtown core valued between $300,00 to $500,000." Wow! That is knowing your expertise.

Some things that you excel at.

Once you figure this out and start marketing the way we teach our clients, you will have to work at finding a way not to make money.

Because you now have a market that is your niche, all the clients in that niche will be attracted to you! The best part is because you know exactly what you are doing there will be people outside of your niche that will follow! This is amazing – people who want to buy condos worth $600,000 will ask you if you can help them too!

This is the power of knowing your market and establishing yourself as an expert.

Let me give you another example. If you are in the weight loss market, instead of saying that you help people lose weight, what if you say, you help women in their 30's to lose weight after pregnancy. Be precise and clear!

When we start any business, we think that we want to have a lot of clients and hence keep our business having to cater to many people at the same time. However, this leads to spreading ourselves over many different areas of our business, and we end up doing no business. That is a big mistake!

I have made that mistake and was striving to get business. Once I had my niche defined, and established myself as an expert in helping existing businesses grow their business online, my business skyrocketed! That does not mean I do not attend to people who want to start their business now and get it online, or businesses that have their online presence and want to enhance it. But they came in after I was established as the expert in one particular area of my expertise.

If you need help figuring out what your niche market should be, or how your business is different, contact me at Amit@Your ProfoundSolutions.com.

3. What is something that your business does that is different than others?

Now that you have your target market and target audience, it is very easy to determine what you do different in this market that no one else does!

Think about your business, your offers and your products. Is there something that you do or offer that has a huge value for clients or potential clients? Is that offered also by your competition?

If you understand your target market problems and offer them solutions, your business will have no competition.

Make a list of 6 things that you can do differently than your competition.

FEATURE	MY BUSINESS	COMPETITOR
Delivery Time	8 hours	3 hours
Product quality	Good	Good
Customer Satisfaction	8/10	9/10
Value for $ spent	Excellent	Good
Refund Policy	90 days	30 days
Free Sampling	Offered	Not Offered

Making a table like this for your own business will give you an idea of all your competitors, and also give you an idea of what you can focus on as your niche.

Once you know exactly what you specialize in, and focus on that specifically, you will stand out from the competition and hence will get clients that will be your loyal followers.

A quick side note: I do not believe in competition. I believe that there is so much opportunity out there for all of us because we are all different. If you can find your calling, your purpose and your expertise and hone in on that, you will have no competition! Amazing isn't it?

It is true! If you attend any of the networking events that we organize, we have all professionals attend, even from the same field. The reason is that, although their field is the same, their expertise in that field is different. If you start thinking about it like that, there is no fear of competition, and you will start developing an abundance mentality.

So how can you position yourself different than others? What can you offer to your potential clients that no one else is offering? What special qualities or features does your business offer that is unique? Once you establish these, you will have no fear of competition and, in fact, you will not fit into a bucket of professionals but will stand out from all others.

Talk to competition – talk about what their niche is! You can work with them and promote each other!

Feedback from customers as to what they like can be used; cross promote your products to them.

4. Are you 'BRANDED'?

Branding is the most important factor in decision-making for clients. The interesting part of the equation is that they may not even know why they are buying what they are buying. If you ask your customers why they bought what they bought, they may not have a concrete answer for you.

Buying is emotional. We like to think that we buy with our logical minds, but the truth is that we buy emotionally, and we justify the purchase with our logical mind.

If you are in the business of selling your product or service, it is imperative that you understand what appeals to your customers' emotions.

All the big names in the industry, like Coke, Pepsi, McDonalds, have their brand so high that they actually have customers insisting on their brand. There are people that will only use a particular brand, or nothing at all! You may have people that try and convince other people to use your brand instead of some other brand without any monetary benefit to them – just because they love your brand so much. That is ultimate loyalty to a brand!

Types of branding:

There are mainly two types of branding:

- Branding with your own name - in this type of branding you would use your personal name to create your brand. Typically sportsmen, musicians, singers and also some top companies have branded themselves with their own names. Examples: KFC (Kentucky Fried Chicken), McDonalds, etc.

    This type of branding adds a personal touch to your business, and people love to do business with people. The major disadvantage to this type of branding is that if you decide to sell your business there may be no takers. For example, if there is a business by the name of Roxanne Smith Janitor Services, if they try to sell their business, it may not be well received in the market.

- Branding with the business name – this is the most common way to brand your business. Example: The Home Depot, Pizza Hut, etc. The disadvantage of having a business name is that the business picks up very slowly because people need to be familiar with the brand name. The advantage is that this is a very lucrative business model if you have intentions of selling your business for huge profit.

More valuable than branding:

Given the facts above that people buy just on the basis of a brand, you may think that branding is the top achievement for any business.

However let me introduce you to another concept, which is more powerful than branding.

Do you know why people take pictures with celebrities? Do you know why top leaders associate with their superiors? Do you know why the top salesman in the company would want his picture with the CEO of the company?

It is all because of UPBRANDING. Upbranding is the elevation of your brand due to your association with a higher brand. Everyone, whatever top position they may be holding, is always looking to upbrand themselves to the next level.

Upbranding works in such a way that if you associate with a person who has a higher brand than you, your brand gets elevated. Because you associate with people of higher brand value, the value of your brand starts to get recognized.

5. Your Target audience

Target audience is a particular group of consumers within the predetermined target market, identified as the targets or recipients for a particular advertisement or message*.

* https://en.wikipedia.org/wiki/Target_audience

Now comes the real and important question – do you know your target audience?

If you have no idea about target audience in your business, that is probably the reason why you're not as successful in your business.

I know that you want to be more successful than you are right now. I know that you have the expertise to earn a 6 figure income easily. How do I know that? Because of all the entrepreneurs that I talk to on a daily basis! You may have so much skill and expertise that you can very well achieve that kind of income, and time to do what you want.

All you need is to channel some of your energy, preferences, and priorities so that you get the best out of yourself. You may need to get in front of your potential clients more often, or get in front of people more often. You may need to increase your presence online or you may need to be more involved in the community.

Now that we have discussed a few options that you may be starting or performing more often, the main shift is your thinking about who you are talking to!

Defining Target Audience is one of the most overlooked aspects of businesses!!!

UNDERSTAND YOUR CUSTOMER

To understand your customer, start by answering these important questions:

- Who are you selling to?
- Why should they buy your product?

DEFINE YOUR TARGET AUDIENCE

The more defined your target audience, the more successful your business! It is as simple as that. This is because you understand them better. You understand what their problems are, what their difficulties are.

- Age, job, family, hobbies and interests.
- Where do they live?
- Give them a name and a picture.
- List common questions, tasks, or frustrations they have.

Describe their attitudes and beliefs.

Here is where you start connecting to your audience emotionally. It is very important that you connect with your audience emotionally, as you will really know your clients better and they will be able to use your services.

- What are their problems and their sources of pain?
- How do they feel about it?
- What are they currently doing to solve them?

HOW DOES IT HELP YOU to know your target audience?

Why is it important? Let me explain: your business cannot and should not be everything to everyone. If your business is the product that is great for everyone to use it may not appeal to anyone.

If you understand your target audience, you will be able to offer exactly the product and service that they need! It will help you TO DESIGN YOUR OFFER/ YOUR PRODUCTS/ YOUR SERVICES!!

When I got clear on my target audience and applied some of the strategies mentioned above, my business started to soar to heights never seen before.

The clearer you are about the clients that you are serving, the better your business will be. In order to teach you the things that you need to know about your target audience, attached is a sheet that'll help you define your target audience.

It is very important that you know your target audience inside out, because these are the people that you're talking to, these are the people you're corresponding with, these are the people that you're sending emails to and so on. So, it may be writing a blog on your website or some content on your website, or even just an email to your list of contacts, or doing a mailout campaign; if you are not talking the language of your target audience you may not be able to connect, and may never get a sale.

The success of any business depends on how well you connect to your customers. If your customers do not understand your language and cannot relate to your information, you may not have a business.

The more you know about your target audience, the more specific that you can get about your target audience, the more success you will get.

This concept is really an easy one to understand but very difficult to implement because when we start our businesses we actually want everyone to buy our product.
You do have to focus your energy on a few things, or even one thing if possible, to excel in the same.

I AM AN EXPERT IN...

Though this may be true when you start a business, you really need to cater to a specific niche in a specific market. Once that market and that niche is happy with your business, your products and your service, you may have no trouble in expanding to different markets.

The biggest mistake that people make is that they focus on getting everybody to buy their products or their services. Let me give you an example. If you are a mortgage broker, you may decide to specialize in people who want to buy their first homes in a specific city. You would want to establish yourself as an expert or an authority in the field of mortgage brokers, as a go-to person for first-time homebuyers' mortgages. If you say you're a specialist in residential mortgages, commercial mortgages, industrial mortgages and all kinds of mortgages offered in the market, you may actually have no customers.

Let us look at another example. If you are in the field of weight loss and nutrition, you want to have a target niche by saying that you are an expert for moms between the age of 35 to 40 who want to lose weight. You may be an expert in helping people lose weight at any age, and both sexes, but for people to get attracted to you, you should select a niche and proclaim your authority.

What do you do?

What you do is such a powerful question. I feel if you take it seriously this question can change your life.

Think about this question, not in terms of just "I am a mortgage broker" or "I am an insurance agent" or "I am an accountant," but a much larger picture.

Remember the trick is always to think big!

How to design the answer:
- Can you tell me in 10 words or less?
- Can you tell me in 10 seconds or less?
- Can you elicit curiosity in me?

Can you help me? (WIIFM)

RULES ABOUT ANSWERING THE QUESTION:
WHO ARE YOU?

- It has to be short.
- It has to elicit curiosity.
- It should tell me what you do.

It should have the words I and you.

TIPS TO HELP YOU ANSWER THE QUESTION:
WHO ARE YOU?

- Talk about how you help people.
- Talk about a void you fill in.
- Talk about an experience that they get.
- Be self-promotional.

Caution: Do not use a or an!!!!

It just puts you in a bucket! It does not create your own identity! It does not distinguish you as a leader as an expert.

Here are some examples:
I help you automate your business.
I help you create passive income
I help you become financially free
I improve your visibility online

CHAPTER 5

Take 'Stress' Out of Marketing

Stress-free marketing for your business

Do you know the major difference between huge, successful corporations and a solo entrepreneur?

Do you know why clients get attracted to a bigger company that has a big brand and a lot of visibility?

Just try to think about the difference between a big real estate company and an independent single real estate agent.

What is the difference between companies like McDonald's, KFC, Red Lobster and the small mom and pop type restaurant?

The main difference is they have a system! Yes, they have a system!

This is the reason you are stuck!!

Do you have a clearly outlined process from the time you first time see the client, a follow-up system to the time of the sale and also a follow-up system that helps you to keep in touch with the client after the transaction is complete?

Do you have a system that educates your client about what you do, and offers lots of value?

How about the services that you are an expert in? Do your clients know exactly what you offer and how you can help them?

Does your system educate your client using the expertise that you have?

The questions mentioned above will give you insight about how you can develop a system to serve your clients and give them the best value so that you become an expert for them. If you continue to follow the system, you will always be the go-to person for any difficulties that your clients have in your niche.

Let us now dive into the various aspects of generating leads, serving them, making a sale and doing the proper follow-up.

Once you master the system and automated it, you are on your way to scale your business up because now you are running on autopilot.

Leads

A lead in a marketing context is a potential sales contact or individuals that expresses interest in your products or services. Leads are typically obtained from your existing customers or as a direct response to your advertising.

There are a number of ways that you can start collecting leads for your business. Let us look at the most successful ways to generate leads:

- Internet leads: Offer something amazing to your target market in exchange for their name and email address. E-books, a free video, reports, a checklist, an e-course, or free newsletter are some of the most popular lead magnets.

- Landing pages: Have a stunning landing page where you offer something of incredible value that they cannot refuse.

- Social Media: Leverage the power of social media by having your presence online on a majority of the social media platforms. The more you understand your target audience, the more you will know where they usually hang out. It is very critical for you to be present where your target audience usually is.

- Face-to-face networking: The value of face-to-face networking is still considered to be the most highly converting practice for lead generation. So feel free to attend as many events as possible, and build your connections.

- YouTube videos: The importance of YouTube videos has grown rapidly in the last few years. Google and YouTube work together, and hence putting a video on YouTube automatically makes it valuable on Google. Do not forget to put in your link for your landing page or your website in the description of the video.

- Blogging: Blogging is truly an art of collecting leads. If your primary focus is collecting leads via blogging, then it's very important that your blogs look very professional and give value to your reader.

- Become a contributor: There are various other websites that are always looking for experts, and expert comments about the questions that people have. You can be a part of a lot of forum discussions so that you can be regarded as an expert.

- Do a joint venture list-building promotion: If you get partnered up with someone that also targets your audience but is in a different niche, you can promote your business to their list and vice versa.

As you are building your leads, try to segment them according to their interests and their requirements. This is very important because when you start your marketing campaigns you should be familiar with the audience that you're talking to.

For example, if somebody has signed up on your list to get information about shoes, then there is no point in sharing information about how to save money when you buy a car.

To start collecting these leads you need to set up the system for collecting them to create a database. This process can be totally automated, using systems and websites that can do this for you. The system that manages your database and sends out emails on your behalf to all your leads is called an auto responder.

There are several auto responders right now that are available for you to try. Some of the most popular ones are Constant Contact, Get Response, AWeber, Mailchimp, etc. If you are looking for more advanced autoresponders with more functions, then your choice would be to go for ActiveCampaign or Infusion Soft.

For the most up-to-date and current auto responder please contact me at Amit@YourProfoundSolutions.com

Sales funnel

The sales funnel is a marketing system where a customer gets introduced to your business, gets value from business and is then channelized to buy product/ products from you.

This is a system that you as a business owner want your customers to go through so that they get properly introduced to your business and are buying your services and products because they love them.

As they continue in the system, they continue to get more value and therefore continue to buy more products from you.

Over a period of time, these customers become so accustomed to your products that they become your product advocates.

If you want a very successful sales funnel, I would recommend that you think of your sales funnel as a relationship funnel.

Step one is when you attract your lead by giving them something for free, and something of great value to them. They are all ready to give you their email address and their name in exchange for a valuable lead magnet.

Step two: now you start to engage them with valuable content that they are interested in. Continue to give them value that helps them in their life or business is saving them money or just making their life easier, depending on what your business is.

Step three: this is where you continue to build relationship and give value. You may even decide to give them some free bonuses just to be more loyal towards you!

Step four: as you have developed a good relationship now there is a lot of trust between you and your lead. You should now be in a position to invite them to check out one of your products or your service for a low price.

This is the step where the rubber meets the road. At this point, if they have been following you and have really developed trust they should be going ahead and buying your product. However, please keep in mind the Pareto principal.

The Pareto principle is a principle, named after economist Vilfredo Pareto that specifies an unequal relationship between inputs and outputs. The principle states that 20% of the invested input is responsible for 80% of the results obtained.*

http://www.investopedia.com/terms/p/paretoprinciple.asp

So please keep in mind that of the 100% effort that you do in your business, 20% of what you do, is going to give you 80% of the success!

Step five: once the customer places an order it's your responsibility to fulfill that in a timely manner, and deliver the exact product that you've promised. If you want to develop that customer into a lifelong customer you need to continue to give them value and have a great follow-up system!

The reason this type of type of marketing works is that it comes with a steady gradient so that the client has an opportunity to know you, to understand you, and also to try some of your products for free!

Hence when they actually have to buy a product from you they already have a very good idea about the quality of the product delivered.

The reason the sales funnel is a very efficient system for you is because the entire process can be automated. Depending on what your lead magnet is, you may actually connect with the client only after they have made a purchase.

Fulfillment

This is a part of the business where the client gets to make a decision whether the money that they paid for the product or service is worth the price. Your entire success of the brand will depend on this last factor.

If you think about a service or product that you have been buying, you might notice that the product that you have is not so unique. It is just an ordinary product. Though there is nothing extraordinary about the product, it is very close to what the vendor had promised you. For this reason, you do not go back to the vendor asking for your money back. For example, when you walk into a fast food restaurant, you see the beautiful pictures of food that is available for sale in that restaurant.

Once you get what you ordered, you will notice that it is not exactly as shown in the picture. But it is also not so much off from what was promised. So you accept that sub-normal product and move on!

The majority of businesses offer you this level of service and products where they are not exactly as promised.

Now think about it – what if you are the business that offers exactly what was promised?! Imagine how happy your customers will be. Imagine how much brand loyalty you will develop.

Now imagine if you deliver and serve something more than what the customers expect. How happy do you think your customers will be now? Imagine the brand loyalty that they will develop for you!!

If you continue to deliver what you promise and, in fact, deliver more than promised each and every time, you will have customers that will promote you over any other brand!

If you look at the customers that buy Apple products or the people that buy Samsung products, all of the people that buy a specific brand do not just buy it because they like the product. They actually love the product so much that not only will they not buy anything else themselves, but they will be the ones promoting, enhancing and uplifting these brands.

Now that you have your system and your sales and marketing funnel defined and set up correctly, you're ready to go out and start promoting your business.

You now have the assurance that, once the customer gets attracted to your funnel, they will be taken care of, nurtured and given so much value that they will start appreciating your brand.

CHAPTER 6

The Profound Way to Promote Your Business

Start promoting your business

Congratulations!!!

You have reached the stage where you are now ready to go in front of your audience and show them your expertise. You have come a long way in structuring your business, defining your business, understanding the core values, and understanding the value you're going to give your clients.

Being clear about your services and products gives you confidence when you're talking to your clients, and also gives you a very clear idea of what you can and cannot do for your clients.

Remember that it is okay to not serve each and every client, and each and every need of the client. As long as you know exactly what you can and cannot provide, you will be a very good business to deal with.

Now that you have decided to promote your business, you have to start thinking about the platforms that you're going to use.

To make a decision about the platforms that you can use, always think about your audience, as to where they usually would be available. For example, if your target audience is high-end business class individuals, you may decide to take up membership at an expensive golf course or a yacht club.

However, if your target audience is teenagers then you may be considering doing a lot of online social media marketing using the latest platforms that are favored by teenagers.

So as you can see, your audience really dictates what platform you use and how you communicate with them.

You have to come up with a budget that you are willing to spend on marketing to get your leads.

2 MOST IMPORTANT CALCULATIONS FOR YOU:

• Cost per lead: since you're going to start promoting your product and spend some money in order for you to get leads, you should have a general idea as to how much it should cost to get you a lead.

The following is the way to calculate your cost per lead:

Total cost for the campaign/ leads you collected

For example: If you collected 20 leads from spending $100 your cost per lead is:

100/20= $5 per lead.

Once you know this number, it is very important to analyze this to decide your budget and your focus of marketing. In the example above, the return is about $5/ day. So if you can get leads at less than $5/lead you are in an excellent business.

2. Customer Acquisition Cost: Out of all the leads that you get, how many actually buy your product or service?

For example let's say that in every 5 leads that you get, 1 person buys your product.

Cost of advertising per sale.

The next step is to take your total expense and divide it by the total people that buy from you.

So to get one person to buy your product, you need 5 leads.

To get 5 leads at $5/lead as per our example, you need to spend $25.

So your per paying client price is $25.

This calculation shows you that your product needs to make a profit of more than $25 for you to use this platform for marketing your products.

Now please read this very carefully.

What we have established is that you are spending $25 to get one sale. How much profit do you make with one sale?

If the profit that you make is more than $25 then you have a winning business model.

Let us look at your business - if you do not have a product or a service that fits into these calculations then you may need to choose a product that has more profit margin, or you may choose to use a platform where the cost of customer acquisition is much lower.

Also important to know is if you have a closer look at your business model this customer paying you $25 dollars profit may just be the beginning of your relationship with the client. If you have a successful business model and a sales funnel, you may have other services, programs and products that you may be able to offer to this client.

We have seen that all successful businesses have a much higher priced back end product to offer to their clients. For example, a business may have a $7 dollar product to begin with and once you have built trust in them, you will either continue to buy from them or they will have a much higher priced item to offer to you that.

These business models are very successful because when the client buys from you the first time they are demonstrating that they trust you. If you deliver what you said you would, and exceed expectations, it is rarely a possibility the they will go and find someone else. That's exactly how you build customer loyalty.

Online Marketing

With the advancement in technology, online marketing seems to take the lead role in any type of marketing today. If you have an online presence, clients are much more likely to buy from you than if you are not found on the Internet.

A lot of purchases are done after researching on the Internet. So if your potential client does a search for your business or looks up your website, the content that they find should be interesting enough for them to actually contact you.

Given the wide variety of Internet today you may have to be visible on a variety of social platforms such as Facebook, Twitter, LinkedIn Pinterest, Tumblr, Reddit, etc.

In fact, clients might find you on these social media platforms. It might be as a result of a blog that you written on LinkedIn, an interesting post that you've done on Facebook, or a tweet on Twitter.

Another reason why social media so powerful today is that it's a social proof. So, as an example, your Facebook page liked by thousands of people is a proof that you are an authentic business and great business to deal with.

The blogs that you write on your website, or that you may write on the other popular blog websites, account for your expertise on the subject that you write about.

The world of online marketing seems to be complex to a lot of people because of all the available options. If you're an entrepreneur and just want to promote your business online at first it may seem overwhelming because you may not know where to start.

We help entrepreneurs to discover their genius and also help them decide their plan for online marketing.

Landing pages

A landing page is any webpage where a visitor arrives or lands on and is asked to input their email address in exchange for some value.

The main intention of a landing page is to only collect the information, and it is important that there is no other distraction to the visitor on that webpage.

The way that a person will land on a landing page is via a link on some other website like Facebook, Twitter ads, LinkedIn ads, etc.

Once the person lands on this page they will be asked for their information – name, email address, phone number, address etc.

The less information that you ask, the more chances to get the visitor to sign up – also called conversion.

The money is in the list (database). So to be successful in your business and improve your audience, it is important that you have and grow your database.

Landing pages are a great way to increase the size of your database.

To attract visitors to your landing page, you may have to offer something of great value to your target audience.

6 RULES FOR A high converting LANDING PAGE:

1. CLEAR CALL TO ACTION — Needs to be a very specific clear call to action.

2. SIMPLE IS BETTER: With landing pages, you do not want to confuse your potential client with lot of information. Keep it really simple!

3. CLEAR AND CONCISE — The message on your landing pages needs to be clear and concise. Because the only intention of the landing page is to collect information, you do not want too much information on that page.

4. Only ask for Name and Email address: I usually only ask for email and first name. If you ask for too much of their information at this first contact, they may be very discouraged to give you any information. I always ask for the name as I want to personalize their emails later on!

5. No navigation tools please: On the landing page, do not give your clients options to click at 70 other places. There should be only one button that they click to get their value once they have put in their name and email address.

6. Keep it 'above the fold': Your offer should be visible right when the clients open your page. They should not have to scroll down to check more information. This is because most people will not. Your content

has to very catchy and attention grabbing above the fold, and also give clients the opportunity to give their email address and name.

WHAT HAPPENS NEXT?

The way it works is that your landing page is linked with an auto responder (automatic emailing system). The moment the person puts in their name and email address and clicks the call to action button, there are two things that happen.

One is that they receive what they have signed up for, but more importantly, they get added to your database so that you can keep communicating with them in the future about more offers and promotions.

Now that you have their email address and name, you can continue to give them value. It is said that you typically need about 7 contacts with an individual to get a sale.

To get the latest and best software to create landing pages please contact me so I can send you some information.

Please write to me at Amit@YourProfoundSolutions.com.

Keeping in touch with your clients

Now that you have your client's contact information you can now keep in touch with them on a regular basis. It is very critical that you keep sending information that is relevant, interesting and of tremendous value to them.

The next and the most popular question in this type of email marketing is how many times to send emails to clients. I know you would love a solid a concrete answer; however, in this case the answer is 'it depends.'

The only reason is that it depends on your target market and your audience.

The average is about 1 email / week. This is because you need to keep in touch with your clients on a regular basis. You need to give so much value and information that you are always the go-to person if they have any question or concern about something that you specialize in.

If you are a service or product that is not used on a regular basis, then the frequency could be lower. However, I do not recommend any less than 1/ month. If you do keep in touch with your clients less than that, they may actually forget you.

The emailing system software that you use has a section that gives you a detailed analysis of who opened your email, how many times, when and if they clicked the link that you sent them in the email. It is important that you have a look at this analysis; however, do not be too carried away or alarmed when you see the number of opens for the campaign that you have sent. It is important to understand that it does not really matter. Your clients may not have the time, and may not need you at that time, to actually open and read your email at that time. However, by sending an email to them you are letting them know that you care about them and that you're there for them if they need you at any point in time.

I believe the main reason why you would send an email to your clients is to remind them that you will be available for them when they need your services.

From your perspective, it's truly a remarkable away to keep in touch with your clients using an automated system. These emails are generally set up through the system and only need to be set up once. Once you have created these emails and decided on the frequency, the system keeps sending them to your entire database. It's done! Now whenever you add a new person to your database the email starts going out automatically with the exact same sequence that you have set up.

Do not be worried about sending out too much information or sending out information too frequently. Because if you're sending valuable information, inspirational messages, emails that actually educate clients, then clients actually want your email do be delivered on a regular basis!

I personally use this system on a regular basis, not just through landing pages but also through the contacts that I develop. So, for example, if I go to a networking event and I'm able to connect with a couple of people with whom I have developed a good relation, I put their name and email address in my database. The moment I put that name and email in my database my first email welcoming my new contact goes out!

In addition to these automated emails you may decide to send emails to your database, depending on some of the current events that might be happening. For example New Year's, Thanksgiving, Easter holidays.

I have seen very good results with sending good information to all my clients. There might be clients on your list to whom you keep sending information, and suddenly after two years they might call you with some questions that they have. For even though you may not have been in touch with them personally because your emails was sent to the automated system on a weekly basis, the client feels that you keep in touch with them on a regular basis. That's the magic of automated email marketing!

Email communication content

Content always seems to be an important concern for a lot of businesses. I truly believe that this is a very genuine consideration. All the correspondence that you're sending is based on it being very valuable and relevant to your clients. So it is critical that the information you send out is the original.

Key factors about content creation:

1. Be original: as an expert in your field, you have so much information to share with people so that whatever you share will be original.

2. Create powerful headlines: do you know that in the copyright world, the person who writes the headline actually gets paid more than the person who writes the entire article? This fact will tell you the importance of headlines for all your contents. It goes for subject lines for all your emails. Your clients may only open your emails if they have a very catchy or interesting subject.

3. Clarity of information: the content that you create for your clients should be very easy to understand, and grammatically correct. The content that you are sharing is a reflection of your knowledge and your brand.

4. Accuracy of information: all the content that you create has to be authentic, and accurate information has to be provided to your clients.

5. Encourage participation: always feel free to encourage people to participate in your article, comment about how they feel about the article, and also ask them for feedback about the content that you have presented.

6. Stories: stories have been shown to elicit maximum interest and get maximum reader attention. Especially if the story is a real life story, that the reader can relate to on some level. Short stories convey a message that probably long descriptions and explanations would not be able to do.

7. Direct: in today's fast-paced environment people generally prefer direct content. They usually do not want the content repeated, nor do they want content that goes round and round without explaining the central idea.

8. Updated content: always make sure that the content you are creating is up-to-date. This is very important because it shows to your reader that you keep up with the times.

9. Use video: using video seems to be one of the best strategies today. People love to watch more than read. If your content has a lot of matter, generally people would like to see that in the form of a video.

10. Frequent: remember to be sending out information and updating your clients on a frequent basis.

If you are not good at writing content or if you feel that you do not have enough time to do that, you can always find good writers to do it for you.

You can hire professional writers to write emails or hard blogs for your website. If you like a particular writer you may wish to hire him or her to do content creation for you on a regular basis.

Content that you create can be used on various websites to blog and create links back to your website. Google loves go to content and so does the majority of the blog sites. So if you are unable to create great content but you are able to hire someone to create great content for you, you will have tremendous followers on social media platforms.

Importance of networking

Motivational speaker Jim Rohn famously said that we are the average of the five people we spend the most time with.

Your network is your net worth: Association with others that are like-minded. Association is really where it all happens. If you have powerful people that you know, you can get a lot of things done in a very short period of time.

Excellent tip on networking: When I started attending networking events, I used to be very apprehensive about who I was going to meet, what I was going to say, what they were going to think, and so forth. Repeatedly going to events has definitely made me more comfortable. But the most important thing that helped me was a change in my attitude. I totally took my focus off me! I was not the topic of discussion. It was all about the person that I was talking to. I became genuinely interested in what the other person was doing, and in their product or services. Due to this approach, people automatically started getting involved in what I was doing. People wanted to know what I was doing and wanted to work with me! What an amazing strategy. Be genuinely interested in others!

Offline marketing – newspapers, radio, magazines – go where your target audience is.

Though online marketing is the buzz word today, off-line marketing still has quite a big role to play. How often do you receive a greeting card in the mail? If you want to stand out from your competition then you will have to make a little bit more effort. This may involve doing something more for your client than what any of your competitor may be doing. For example, go to the market, buy greeting cards, write out your wishes, and actually mail them to your clients.

Newspapers today still have a lot of readership and grab the attention of a lot of readers through their creative advertising. Magazines and any other print media also utilize a lot of advanced strategies to attract clients, to actually lead to their brochures and information booklets.

Radio is another form of communication between you and your potential clients. There are various ways you can promote yourself on the radio. You can actually host a video show or you can pay someone to go on their show.

You're able to buy timeslots on radio. Different stations have different duration of programs. For example a 30-minute program could have about eight minutes of commercials and 22 minutes of talk time for you. The radio station usually decides the commercials and you get to do your 22 min talk between those commercials. It's important to keep the audience engaged by giving important information. Because it is on radio your program should have some entertainment value. It may be offered in terms of some interesting stories, some current incidents, or playing some music that the audience would love.

The other way to do it is by sponsoring a program so that the person conducting the program will say that you are the sponsor of the event and also may play your commercial. If you decide to do it this way as a part of that event, you may also request the organization that you're sponsoring to interview you for 5 to 10 minutes during the event.

Mail campaigns are also very popular in off-line advertising. You have your brochure or your flyer that goes out either inside the newspaper, or is actually mailed out to a huge database of people that live in a specific neighbourhood.

You may also opt for mailing out your brochure to a list of addresses that you can buy. The costs involved are usually higher as you are paying for buying the database, brochure printing and the mailing costs.

Sometimes it is a good idea to partner up with someone who wants to target the same area but is in a completely different business. You can outsource this type of advertising to companies that actually do the mail outs for you as they already have other businesses that can share the cost. You get to select the space that you want to advertise and, depending on how big your ad is, you get charged. The best thing to do in these types of ads is to give an amazing offer to your audience. Like 50% off a service, free consultation or free report, etc.

The main intent of this advertisement is to attract the clients to contact you. The benefit is the cost could be low for this type of advertising, but the disadvantage is that you are advertising to a non-targeted audience.

CHAPTER 7

The Profound Way to Atract Clients to Your Business

Online promotions

Now that you have your landing page and your auto responder set up, you're already to start advertising online.

You may choose to advertise online because the majority of the time you can target your audience exactly according to your niche market. Facebook has one of the most advanced advertising models. The amount of customization that you can do to get a specific targeted audience to your website or your landing page is very well defined.

To advertise online you need to have a very compelling offer that your potential clients would be interested in. The ad that you place can be in the form of text, an image, a banner ad, or video commercial. Video commercials have recently seen the maximum return on investment for your advertising dollars. Please make sure that your advertisement is speaking to your target audience to get maximum conversions. It's important to speak the language of your customer so that they get attracted to your business.

There are several websites where ads can be placed. Facebook, twitter, Google ad words, LinkedIn, tumblr, Pinterest etc. have big huge platforms for advertising. Depending on where you think your target audience hangs out, you can decide on your advertising platform.

The main advantage of advertising online is the feature of customization, or targeting your audience.

If you structure your ad correctly, and also set it up correctly using very specific parameters, you will find tremendous success with Facebook ads. All these ads will direct people to go to your landing page, where they give you their name and email address. This gets added to your database and the communication with your new client begins.

In Facebook ads you can target age, sex, the occupation, profession, interests, marital status, address, etc. As you can see, if you know your audience, Facebook will help you target very specifically to your audience. Based on your selection, Facebook will also tell you how many clients you will be able to reach with your ad. Facebook also has suggestions for you based on your primary selections.

One of the models that Facebook uses is called Pay-Per-Click. What that essentially means is that anytime a person clicks on your ad you get charged. If you have structured the ad well, your pay per click should be very low. If you find you're spending too much you may have to consult Facebook add specialists, who can help you advertise more aggressively but within a constrained budget.

If you need help with any of your online ad placements you can give me a call. I can direct you to the right person, who can help you put down ads correctly, and even with a lower budget you will reach more audience. Please contact me at Amit@YourProfoundSolutions.com.

Website

Domain names selection

Wow, what an exciting time for your business! Selection of your domain name!!

I remember when I selected the domain for my website it took me about a week!

To help you make it easier to select your domain name, here are a few tips:

1. You have to decide what your domain name is going to be about: your domain name could have these three options based on how you want to brand yourself:

- Your name: if you have decided to brand yourself with your own name, then your domain name will be your name.com. The advantage of doing it this way is that it's totally unique to you. Your audience is very clear as to who this business belongs to;

117

however, the disadvantage is that the business is not transferable. I know what you must be thinking- why would I want to transfer the business I'm just opening it up right now? You are right; you're just opening it up right now, but if you have structured the business correctly and are going to put in the required effort, your business is going to flourish and expand. In the future, you may decide to sell off this business and take up a new business!

If your business is with your own name it cannot be easily transferred to another person because your name is your brand.

- The other way to brand yourself is with your company name. The disadvantage of this type of domain name is that, because your company is new, nobody will know your company's name. People will have to get familiar with your company name before they buy products from you. You might find the success rate of this type of company name to be slow; however, once people recognize your company name, this is the best option to opt in for. The big advantage of this is that you can sell your domain name and your business to another person to make huge profits.
- You can have keywords of your business as your domain name. So, for example, if you sell chairs then www.bestchairs.com could be your domain name. The disadvantage is that you do not have a real brand. The advantage of this is that when people are searching for the best chairs, the chances of you coming up on the search results are very high.

eBook

One of the fastest ways to promote yourself is by using an e-book that you have written; that you have put together with your expertise. It does not have to be a full-length book or even in a digital format. Many in my network have written their first e-books from collecting all the blogs that they have written on their websites. The main concept and the title of the book has to be clearly defined, and a solution should be offered in the book.

As long as the book is able to deliver what it says it will deliver to the reader, I believe it is a great product to advertise and promote.

E-books are also one of the favorite lead magnets (something that you give away to get clients' information).

Webinars

The concept of using webinars is not new; however, I am surprised as to how few people utilize this crucial tool. If you're an expert in your niche and if you want to promote yourself, giving value to others, this is one of the most important tools that I would encourage you to use. Today there are so many software programs and websites that you can use to create successful webinars. Some of these are paid but some are actually free.

Social Media

Social media is such a huge topic now, that an entire book has been written on this topic alone. The importance of social media is so huge that any successful company has to change their marketing strategies to adapt to the changes in social media if they want to still be in business in five years. There have been companies like Blockbuster and BlackBerry that did not adapt to the changes in technology and trends. At their peak, these companies were considered to be unstoppable. My son, who is five years old, does not even know what these companies are. That just tells you how important it is to keep changing your advertising medium, your promotional material and your marketing strategies, in order to get to the top or to keep you at the top.

Online Membership Sites

If you have organized your database to have clients and potential clients that are interested in your services or products, the next best thing to do is have an online membership model where your clients can hear you and meet you in action every week or every month. Remember that there is so much competition out there, that if you are not able to service your clients for as little as one week they may find another business that provides them with a similar service or product.

I find that this is one of the best ways you can offer valuable coaching, mentoring or training to potential clients and students.

It enables the client to get your specialized training to an online membership paid website to access your expertise.

I think it is important to draw the line where people have to pay to get the information that they need. Sometimes we are too gentle to ask for money, but trust me, if you believe that you have something that gives incredible value to your client they will be glad to pay you for what you have to offer. Also, if it is going to make them prosper and make them more money, I do not see anything wrong in charging for giving them value.

Research is shown that if a particular program cost money, the commitment level is much higher than if it is free. Furthermore, the more expensive the program, the greater the commitment!

SEO (Search engine optimizations)

Google searches and results

Today there are more than 1 billion websites on the Internet. So if you start up your website today and put it up there it gets lost in this big jungle called Internet.

Whenever your potential clients do a search for you or your products, it is very critical that you show up as one of the first in the search results, or at least on the first page of the search results.

All search engines like Google, Bing, Yahoo, AOL etc. use a specific system for determining which websites will show up when anyone searches for a specific term.

With the growing popularity of the Internet it is a given that your potential clients will research you on the Internet before they do business with you.

Have you done your name search on Google recently?

Go to Google.com, put in your name and just see what comes up. Is it something relevant that you're doing right now? Is it something that you want customers to see? Next try putting your business name into the search bar and look at the results. You can also try the product and service that you are trying to establish yourself in, and see what comes up. SEO means that your website is optimized to show up on these search engine results. There are specific rules and systems that need to be followed for your website to show up.

These search results are so powerful that it is said that if you can rank on the first page of Google it's very hard not to make money.

SEO is really an expertise and needs good training and knowledge for doing it.

Let me share with you 8 different ways to increase your chances of showing up on search results:

1. Have a good domain name: The domain name is your website address. You may either have your website address as the name of your brand or the service that you offer. For example, our domain name is YourProfoundSolutions.com, which is of course our brand name.

If you decide to use your services in your domain name you could do that as well. Example: GtaRentToOwn.com would be a website that offers rent to owns in Greater Toronto Area(GTA)..

2. Just like a book, a website also has a title and a subtitle. It is important that you use the correct title, and an appropriate subtitle that is relevant to your business.

3. Keywords: this is a set of words that are searched on the Internet. Google offers tools such as Google keyword tool for you to get an idea about which keywords you can use for your website, your blogs, or any other marketing that you do.

4. Content: Content is still the king! You must have relevant and original content on your website.

5. Images and Videos: The more videos and images you have on your website, the better it is. The reason videos and images are important is because visitors to your website will be on your website much longer, and more often, if they find your website informative and engaging.

6. Social media presence: All your social media profiles should be linked to your website. Look for social media platforms that have lots of traffic and users.

7. Links to your website: Talking about your own business is good, but if other people say great things about your business it's great. Isn't it? That's exactly the way the search engines work. In other words, if you say something on your website it's good; however, if somebody mentions your website on their website and social media platform, that has a lot of value. This is called back linking.

8. Google index: your new website or your existing website should be registered with Google. Google should also know about any other blogs that you write, or pages that you create for your website. You can do this by submitting your site to Google. This is called Google indexing.

Client testimonials

Client testimonials have a higher value today than ever before. Everyone that wants to do business with you, everyone that wants to buy your product or buy your services, will find it of immense value to look at some testimonials from other people who have used your services. Before buying any product they need social proof for success of the product.

You can get them in the form of video testimonials or written testimonials and then post them on Social media.

Use different channels to spread the word – Pinterest/ FB/ Twitter/ Snapchat/ Whats app/ YouTube/ Vimeo/ Tumblr/ Wordpress blogs, to reach a larger and more spread out audience.

I specialize in improving your visibility online through various methods, so contact me if you would like to discuss how I can help you. Contact me through my website YourProfoundSolutions.com.

CHAPTER 8

The Grand Take-Off

Welcome to the 'ANALYSIS PARALYIS PHASE!'

The End of Procrastination... Forever!!!

As an entrepreneur do you find yourself busy? Do you find you have lots of ideas and lots of things that you want to do, but you do not get enough time to do those things?

When I met my coach Raymond Aaron, he taught me a phenomenal principle that I am going to share with you that changed my whole life! I cannot describe what changes took place in my life. The changes that I experienced using this one single step were so profound that it changed my whole perspective about how to get things done and achieve my goals.

As you are reading this book, you probably have in your mind a list of about 20 to 25 things that you need to do. Now answer the following question as the answer will shock you! For how long have these been in your mind as things to do? Let's discuss this in a little bit greater detail and let me explain you. Things that you have on your to-do list have been sitting there for quite some time probably a very long time. And the reason why they are not getting done, the reason why you have them on your to do list, the reason you're procrastinating to do those things is and here comes the giant secret you don't want to do it.

The only way you can get things done and achieve your goals in an amazingly fast way is to DELEGATE either your entire to do task or at least a part of that task!!

Yes that's one of the giant secret that has made such a profound effect in my business. I had a lot of resistance to accept this first. My be like you I thought that I can do a much better job than outsourcing it to someone else. Which may be true, however, it is better to get it done by someone else even though it is about it is not exactly what you wanted to do, because if you were the one doing it you would not have done it at all

This principle though easy is not an easy one to accept and implement. I myself have some challenges that I'm still working on to apply this principle 100% of the time. However every aspect that I have applied this principle I have seen gigantic progress in my personal life and my business.

You may have to look at your business and identify the areas that you are good at and the areas that you're not good at. The sooner you delegate these aspects of your business, the sooner you will make money and be successful in your business. Find out which aspects of your business marketing, sales, order, delivering are you a extremely good at and do only those things!! Other factors that are needed to get your business going should be outsourced/ delegated or bartered.

Let me give you an example: how would you feel if your heart replacement surgeon was also doing the billing and accounting for the clinic, was also involved in setting up your appointment times and arranging the logistics of your hospital stay? It sounds funny, doesn't it? You really want the heart specialist surgeon to do a good job of surgery, advise you about medication, and have a follow-up just related to the surgery.

Let's talk about another example. Think about Celine Dion. Do you think she organizes the venues or the publicity for her events? She only does what she does best, performing.

Now think about your business. Think about the small components of your business that you do on a daily basis. Now start thinking about some of the things that you're extremely good at in your business. Some of the things that are just irreplaceable that only you can do. Now everything that is left behind and everything that is on that list still needs to be done, needs to be delegated.

The Vital components of business - Teaming up

GET YOUR TEAM READY

Identify where you need help:
- Marketing
- Sales
- Delivery

Describe the biggest challenge that you experience in this specific domain.

If you could wave a magic wand and attract any partner that you want in your business, what kind of partner would that be?

Team up:

Do you know that the concept of self-made millionaire is actually true? It really means that the person yes worked very hard worker very smart and went up to that level to become a millionaire however there are lots of people and friends and team that helps him or her to get there. The fact cannot be ignored that the person needed some coaching some mentoring so my advice some form of help on the way to become a millionaire.

I have met several millionaires in my life I'm not one millionaire has told me that dated it all by themselves not even one. In fact all Old Dominion there's always give credit to their team that appliance their colleagues that made it successful for them to reach new heights.

Usually the only people who do not have a team are solo entrepreneurs. Think about that for a moment if you're in your business all by yourself and working hard to do everything you can and working without a team how far can you going your business. Let's look at some examples if you want to succeed as a real estate investor you must have a phenomenal mortgage broker a great realtor a dependable property management team and so on

If you want to run an online business you must have a good website developer, a personal manager of social media, and a person who does blogs for you.

CHAPTER 9

How Do You Grow From Here Now?

Evaluate your outcomes

Do some statistical data analysis to grow more.

Ask your customers for feedback: This is the most valuable and crucial feedback that you can get. Ask your customers what is working for them and what needs improvement. A lot of businesses do not ask for feedback, as they are afraid to find out!

I believe that if they do that, they will at least know, and will be able to correct it or change it so that not only the present clients will be happy but the ones that are going to join in as new well also be very happy and satisfied.

Feedback is important, even from your employees, so that you understand what's keeping them happy and what's not working. Generally people are very honest and will give you a quick feedback, and then it's up to you to decide if you want to make any changes in your business.

The Pareto Principle

Have you heard of the Pareto Principle?

The Pareto principle is a principle, named after economist Vilfredo Pareto, that specifies an unequal relationship between inputs and outputs. The principle states that 20% of the invested input is responsible for 80% of the results obtained. Put another way, 80% of consequences stem from 20% of the causes; this is also referred to as the "Pareto rule" or the "80/20 rule."!*

http://www.investopedia.com/terms/p/paretoprinciple.asp

If we decide to use this principle in our business, it means that we're getting 80% of our business from 20% of the clients.

Wow!! Isn't that something worth noting? Isn't that something to consider when you're proving service to your clients? Have you identified those 20% of clients that give you 80% of your business? Now that you know this principle, would you treat the 20% differently?

When I discovered the secret, it really made me understand the importance of those special clients. I have changed my business model to serve that 20% in the best possible way. I do make it a point to give them special considerations and special discounts for being my regular clients.

The Pareto Principle does not give any indication about the numbers that this would work for. The Pareto Principle would work for 10 people the same way as it would for 2000 people. Haven't you seen that all the time, wherever you go, you see the same numbers? At your workplace, 20% of the people are the ones that work really hard and the rest are not working that hard.

If you own your own business, you will realize that 20you're your employees work really hard and get things done!

Wow!! Imagine if we could rid of the 80% that is not working! It would give our business a whole different perspective. That is exactly what successful companies do all the time. We therefore see that the hiring and firing rate for a lot of major companies is very high.

Celebrate: How was your celebration for you last success?

A lot of entrepreneurs miss this factor, as they get busy in "doing" things for their business. They are working harder and harder each minute in their business. The trick is to work on your business, and not in your business.

Even if you get a "small' success, CELEBRATE IT!! In reality, there is no such thing as a small success. All successes are steps that you take to achieve your BIG success!

CHAPTER 10

Bigger Than Yourself

Giving back

Once you have reached the level where you have achieved huge success, where do you go from here?

I believe it's now the time for giving back. Even though you may have been giving back all along, and that would have been a reason why you achieved so much success, you now have the opportunity to do more.

You may decide to give your time, your money, your expertise, or share your resources with others that are looking for growth and empowerment.

It is also very gratifying for you to give back as it uplifts you as an individual and enhances your spirit.

There are so many different ways to start giving back. Let us explore a few:

Teach

Once you have achieved a certain level of success in your business, you can definitely expand your business in the same direction or in some other related niche by scaling it up. You may also choose to add other avenues to the same business that can give value to a lot of people who are trying to achieve what you have already achieved.

Examples of this may be:

- Group coaching: Group coaching refers to training sessions where you train many people at the same time. They can be arranged in a live setting or in a webinar. This form of coaching resonates with a lot of people because it gives a lot of value to the end-user at a very affordable price.

- One-on-one coaching: One-on-one coaching can also be done on the phone, in person, or in a webinar or Skype. In the one-on-one session you actually give a one-on-one customized plan to your client, about how they can achieve what they want to achieve. Though this may be a little more expensive, the return on this form of investment for the client is way more than in a group setting.

- Masterminds: Masterminds are usually misunderstood. You might think of masterminds as a group of people coming together and having a discussion. Mastermind actually means that you have at least a couple of people who are super specialists solving the problems that are being discussed in the group. It is not a platform where individuals express what they think would work, or give their opinions on the subject. Mastermind groups will only work when you have a super successful person in that specific business attending your meeting, and others wanting advice on that topic.

- Retreats: I have had the honor and privilege to attend one of Raymond Aaron's retreats, which was on a cruise ship to the Bahamas. The impact of such learning is so gigantic that it cannot be expressed in words. You have to attend, enjoy, learn and apply the teachings of the master in order for you to see huge results. The learning that happens on events like this is far beyond the education in urban hotels. The main reason is because we were in such a luxury and away from home, with no cell phones and no distractions, so we could concentrate and absorb the high level of coaching and teaching.

Your Coaching Programs

One of the best ways to spread the knowledge and information is to have coaching programs for the people that want to learn from you.

The amount of coaching programs available today is so vast that you can take up coaching for any specialization that you choose.

There are several variations of coaching programs. And now due to the Internet, the forms of coaching also have taken several routes.

The following gives you some ideas if you want to start your own coaching program.

Because, generally, coaching is expensive, you may not start the client directly on a coaching program. They would have to know you and trust you enough to actually take up your coaching programs.

In the sales cycle, coaching programs, you get either go for one-on-one time or group coaching with the master of that program.

Jump-start call: If your client has accepted coaching with you, it is generally a good idea to do a quick startup call. To get the maximum results for your coaching program, it is very important that you understand the needs, the goals, and the expectations of your client. This is an important step because if there is any misunderstanding you may be able to rectify the problem right before it arises.

Generally it helps to offer different tiers within your coaching program. Your clients may be at different levels financially, as well as in their business, and hence different level packages will attract different clients.

For example, if you have a client that is already familiar with the business that they're doing, and need some help to take it to the next level, they may need more one-on-one coaching, which is customized to them. On the other hand, if you have a client that is just starting, or a client that does not know where to get started, they may be more open to something more basic to start working on some ideas.

Offering different packages and different tiers also gives your clients the opportunity to try out a smaller package, and if they love your style of teaching and your method they may wish to continue with you with a bigger package.

I help entrepreneurs design their packages to be offered to clients, so that they're giving a lot of value, and also taking care that their clients are getting more than what they paid for.

All features and benefits of the programs that you offer should be clearly defined. It is also important that you define the start date and the ending of those programs.

As clients sign up, they have a very good idea what to expect in their coaching sessions. This helps you, as well as the client.

All clients in your coaching program should have access to you via phone, email, Facebook groups etc.

If you have other coaches as a part of your team, it should be made clear to the client who will be taking care of them on a regular basis.

Due to the advancement in technology, you can now have your coaching students connect to you more often with either Skype or regular webinars.

Ideally, it would be a good idea to connect with your client at least two times a week. This contact does not have to be an in-person contact, but it may be a simple email to make sure that they are on track with the program to be successful

Follow-up system: I have been in a lot of coaching programs, and one of the most common complaints of coaching students is that the follow-up component of these coaching programs is very poor. If you want your coaching program to stand out from the rest, this is one of the best tips I can give you. Have a fantastic long-term follow-up system that will keep your clients on the program, and will ensure that not only will they become successful, but they will stay successful!

Leaving a legacy

I was recently at the business meeting, talking to a friend about leaving a legacy. He said that he has two daughters and one son in university, so he felt that he has met all his obligations and is leaving a legacy. I cringed at this thought, as that is not my idea of leaving a legacy. To me leaving a legacy is much more than that.

Your Profound Success

Leaving a legacy to me means the need or the desire to be remembered by other people about your work and your contributions to the world. Leaving a legacy is much more than just leaving a few dollars in your bank account, or leaving a couple of pieces of property to your children.

Leaving a legacy refers to the number of people that benefited due to your existence, your teachings, your ideas, your encouragement, your planning, your execution and so on.

How important is leaving a legacy for you?

There are a few incredible ways to leave a legacy for generations to come. Who better can we learn from than the master- Jim Rohn?

Jim Rohn: This Is How You Leave a Legacy

Jim Rohn, the philosopher who has left an indelible legacy of time-proven principles and wisdom, shares his nice principles for making an impact.

"You know me, I am a philosopher. I love principles. Yes, actions are great and I talk about them regularly, but the important stuff is what lies underneath—the principles," Rohn says.

149

Here are the principles he says we must commit to in order to leave the legacy we desire:

1. Life is best lived in service to others.

This doesn't mean that we do not strive for the best for ourselves. It does mean that in all things we serve other people, including our family, co-workers and friends.

2. Consider others' interests as important as your own.

Much of the world suffers simply because people consider only their own interests. People are looking out for number one, but the way to leave a legacy is to also look out for others.

3. Love your neighbour even if you don't like him.

It is interesting that Jesus told us to love others. But he never tells us to like them. Liking people has to do with emotions. Loving people has to do with actions. And what you will find is that when you love them and do good by them, you will more often than not begin to like them.

4. Maintain integrity at all costs.

There are very few things you take to the grave with you. The number one thing is your reputation and good name. When people remember you, you want them to think, "She was the most honest person I knew. What integrity." There are always going to be temptations to cut corners and break your integrity. Do not do it. Do what is right all of the time, no matter what the cost.

5. You must risk in order to gain.

In just about every area of life you must risk in order to gain the reward. In love, you must risk rejection in order to ask that person out for the first time. In investing you must place your capital at risk in the market in order to receive the prize of a growing bank account. When we risk, we gain. And when we gain, we have more to leave for others.

6. You reap what you sow.

In fact, you always reap more than you sow—you plant a seed and reap a bushel. What you give you get. What you put into the ground then grows out of the ground. If you give love you will receive love. If you give time, you will gain time. It is one of the truest laws of the universe. Decide what you want out of life and then begin to sow it.

7. Hard work is never a waste.

No one will say, "It is too bad he was such a good, hard worker." But if you aren't they will surely say, "It's too bad he was so lazy—he could have been so much more!" Hard work will leave a grand legacy. Give it your all on your trip around the earth. You will do a lot of good and leave a terrific legacy.

8. Don't give up when you fail.

Imagine what legacies would have never existed if someone had given up. How many thriving businesses would have been shut down if they quit at their first failure? Everyone fails. It is a fact of life. But those who succeed are those who do not give up when they fail. They keep going and build a successful life—and a legacy.

9. Don't ever stop in your pursuit of a legacy.

Many people have accomplished tremendous things later on in life. There is never a time to stop in your pursuit of a legacy. Sometimes older people will say, "I am 65. I'll never change." That won't build a great life! No, there is always time to do more and achieve more, to help more and serve more, to teach more and to learn more. Keep going and growing that legacy!

These are core principles to live by if you want to become the kind of person who leaves a lasting legacy.

**http://www.success.com/article/rohn-this-is-how-you-leave-a-legacy

Wouldn't you want to leave a legacy to help people, not just in your generation but also for generations to come?

SUMMARY

It was my pleasure to write this book and I am sure that you as an entrepreneur will value the information in this book.

The reason I wanted to share this information is because when I started in my business, there was no one to guide me for my business online needs.

I always thought online marketing as a big huge complex jungle, which has no beginning and no end. Online seemed very overwhelming but at the same time online marketing cannot be ignored as that is the wave of the future.

A lot of entrepreneurs that we talk to have the same problem and hence I decided to write a book to start making you aware about certain basic processes that are involved in marketing online.

I wanted to keep the book simple because I wanted to focus on a variety of aspects and not just online marketing. An entrepreneur is not just looking at one aspect of their business and hence such a simple book was important.

Entrepreneurs are struggling to create their online identity and that's where we help them make it possible.

I want to encourage you to go through this book again and again as you will get some nuggets each time you read it.

I am so blessed that I have Raymond Aaron as my co-author. Raymond is a phenomenal teacher and coach. To get his coaching and being his student for a long time now really gave me the courage and inspiration to write this book.

Loral Langemier, who is known as the Millionaire maker, has written the foreword for my book! That is one the most fascinating feature of this book!

It's truly my greatest honour to write this book for you my dearest reader, as I wanted to share some insights about how to create and promote your business online.

Please feel free to contact me if you have any questions about your business.

Email: Amit@YourProfoundSolutions.com